THE
MACMILLAN
BOOK
OF BONSAI

D0709180

HORST DAUTE

THE
MACMILLAN
BOOK
OF BONSAI

Translated by Carole Ottesen

COLLIER BOOKS
MACMILLAN PUBLISHING COMPANY
New York

COLLIER MACMILLAN PUBLISHERS
London

Macmillan Publishing Company
866 Third Avenue, New York, N.Y. 10022
Collier Macmillan Canada, Inc.

Title of the original German edition:
BONSAI: Pflege und Anzucht japanischer Zwergbäume
© 1980 BLV Verlagsgesellschaft mbH,
München

Library of Congress Cataloging-in-Publication Data
Daute, Horst.
    The Macmillan book of Bonsai.

    Includes index.
1. Bonsai.   I. Title.
SB433.5.D38   1986   635.9'772   85-26985
ISBN 0-02-062660-6

10 9 8 7 6 5 4 3 2 1

Printed in Germany

Contents

7   **Introduction**

9   **Origins and Fundamentals**

What Is Bonsai? 9
Bonsai Are Not Stunted
    Trees 10
Bonsai, Past and Present 10
Religion and Philosophy 11
Bonsai in the Western
    World 11
What Makes a Good
    Bonsai? 13
Bonsai Versus Natural
    Trees 15
How Long Does a Bonsai
    Take? 15
Plants That Lend Themselves
    to Bonsai 16
Favorite Bonsai Plants 18

19 **Care and Cultivation**

Collecting in the Wild 19
Nursery Plants 21
Bonsai from Seed 23
Bonsai from Cuttings 25
Bonsai from Grafts 28
Bonsai from Air-Layering 30
Bonsai Containers 31
Soil and Soil Mixtures 32
Potting and Repotting 34
Watering 38
Fertilizers 40
Bonsai Aren't Houseplants 41
Diseases and Pests 43
Tools 44

46 **Styling**

Goals and Reasons 46
Most Popular Bonsai
    Styles 48

How Styles Are Trained 60
Styling with Wire and Cord 61
Shoot Pruning 66
The Leaf-Cutting Method 68

71 **Purchased or Home-Grown**

The Purchased, Finished
    Bonsai 71
Bonsai for the Home 72
How Much Should a Bonsai
    Cost? 74
Where and How to Buy 75
Reworking a Nursery
    Bonsai 77

80 **A Guide to Cultivating the Most Popular Bonsai Plants**

Needle Evergreens 80
Deciduous Trees 90
Flowering and Fruit-Bearing
    Plants 101

109 **Unusual Forms**

Miniatures 109
Giant Bonsai 110
A Bonsai Garden 110
Bamboo and Herbaceous
    Bonsai 112
Saikei 114

116 **Bonsai Terms**

119 **Bonsai Societies**

120 **Index**

Introduction

During the Bicentennial in 1976, Japan's gift to the United States was a magnificent collection of bonsai. The oldest, a Japanese black pine, came from the Japanese imperial household, where it had flourished for more than three centuries.

Being able to see outstanding examples of bonsai in this country gave this already popular hobby a great boost. Indeed, bonsai is a kind of gardening whose time has come. In terms of size, portability, and satisfaction, bonsai fits into even a big-city life-style. Grown on the smallest rooftop, balcony, or terrace, bonsai can thrive without a greenhouse, yard help, or a garage full of tools. And the tools that *are* required for the cultivation of these little trees can fit into a small drawer.

Although all bonsai require regular care, maintenance is really quite minimal. One might spend far less time on the cultivation of an entire bonsai forest than on the mowing of a single lawn.

While all gardening employs our aesthetic sense in varying degrees, bonsai goes a step further: In its strictly disciplined horticulture and in its traditional styling of living raw material, bonsai represents a fusion of nature and art.

Trident maple *(Acer buergerianum)* in oval dish, 12 × 16 inches (30 × 40 cm); height, 22 inches (55 cm).

Origins and Fundamentals

What Is Bonsai?

The Japanese term "bonsai" (plural, "bonsai") freely translated means "a tree in a pot," and it refers to both the dwarf plant and the art of creating that plant. (To get the pronunciation just right, the "o" should be articulated deep in the throat.) The basic principle behind bonsai is that certain types of trees and shrubs can be dwarfed by growing them in small, generally flat containers (although dwarfing may not always result), and with years of patience and regular pruning the bonsai gradually takes on its distinctive, miniaturized form.

When we look at a bonsai, it should evoke the image of an aged, gnarled tree shaped by the elements, or perhaps give the impression of a sunlit grove or tiny forest. Whatever the case, ideally the bonsai and its container together should present a unified visual image and be a self-contained biological entity as well.

Needle juniper *(Juniperus rigida),* approximately 40 years old. Ceramic pot, 19×13½ inches (47×33 cm). Total height, 32 inches (80 cm).

Containers
The bonsai's normal growth is restricted because the small pot size limits root growth. The minimal root system provides the barest supply of nutrients, supporting only modest growth. This same phenomenon also may be observed in nature, where trees growing on stony ground or in rock crevices eke out a meager existence, requiring decades to reach only knee height.

Pruning
Another important element in training a bonsai is regular pruning of the shoots and branches. At the same time that pruning works to perfect the shape and placement of the branches, it has an inhibiting effect on root growth. Pruning should be undertaken either annually or once every several years.

Soil Composition
Pot size, pruning, root pruning—all of these factors go hand in hand with the use of special soil individually mixed to suit each type of tree. When chosen correctly, a soil mix will further augment the dwarfing process both above and below ground.

Finally, the effects of sun and wind contribute to the bonsai process, combining to further limit the subterranean water supply. Naturally, this exposure must not be

Origins and Fundamentals

overdone to the point that a plant wilts or withers.

Bonsai Are Not Stunted Trees

It is obvious that the creation of a bonsai is the result of a whole series of practices, and only when they are carried out regularly and correctly is the magic of bonsai possible. Only then can a bonsai—no matter how aged and gnarled it may appear—retain the same health and vigor as its larger relatives in nature.

With a good bonsai, the harmonious relationship of trunk to branches, and above all the fresh and lush appearance of its foliage, are expressions of a healthy and robust state of being.

The Eastern concept of bonsai and the way that our culture has interpreted it are far removed from the comfortable, all-American notion of "mighty oaks." Yet, blithely labeling bonsai as "stunted," or even "deformed," is a knee-jerk reaction to a painstaking process that requires the patience and attention to fine detail of a goldsmith. The creation of a bonsai is no more brutal or unnatural than the pruning of a peach tree or the training of a rose arbor.

Bonsai, Past and Present

Nearly a millenium has passed since the first written mention of bonsai appeared in ancient China. Many old documents still exist with illustrations of little trees growing in pots. In those days only the aristocracy and certain members of the clergy were privy to the secrets of bonsai training. These secrets were passed on to an elect from generation to generation.

Religion and Philosophy

Bonsai is a notion very much a part of Eastern religion in which human beings occupied a very much closer and more harmonious place in nature. They worshiped nature and saw themselves as only one small element of the whole. In that hierarchy trees were observed as having a special role. In the lofty stature of trees, man found a link between heaven and earth, and in their many forms he found a whole range of human feelings and emotions represented. More on this subject later.

Bonsai came to Japan from China at a date now lost to time. It was there that the art of bonsai found fertile ground and flourished, developing into the rich discipline we know today. Practiced for centuries behind the high walls of castles and monasteries, bonsai was

Origins and Fundamentals

eventually taken up as a popular art.

Bonsai, like ikebana, is displayed to perfection in the utter plainness and simplicity of the typical Japanese house or cottage, at its best against a perfectly blank wall. Situated thus, it absorbs the viewer's undivided attention and is more readily appreciated for its form and beauty.

In order to better grasp the spirit of bonsai in Japan, one should understand that in a traditional Japanese house big windows never look toward the outside. Instead, semitransparent paper screens serve to keep the natural, untrammeled surroundings hidden from view, and a bonsai serves as a piece of highly idealized nature, a carefully styled representation of all of nature in concentrated form. In this regard, the bonsai often serves as a focus of meditation for many Japanese. And today, more and more Japanese are taking up bonsai as a leisure activity.

Bonsai in the Western World

Bonsai as a hobby has earned a secure status in the West. Particularly in big cities, where the impersonality of modern life and dissatisfaction in the workplace are on the rise, the need for meaningful and worthwhile leisure time is growing. The expression "green revolution," the result of a general wave of nostalgia, is not an isolated phenomenon.

Among the potted plants, bonsai occupies a position of prestige, especially since it is not merely a disposable ornament to be tossed out when the season is over. The notion that a bonsai's culture demands years or even decades of effort to produce a small work of art that may one day as in Japan be passed on from generation to generation is central to its growing popularity. For those who take up bonsai, the hobby offers meaningful occupation, pleasure, self-realization, and a certain relief from workaday stress.

Origins and Fundamentals

Origins and Fundamentals

What Makes a Good Bonsai?

As with other art forms, over centuries, a rigid discipline of bonsai has evolved. Both the execution of individual components as well as total form of an individual bonsai are judged with centuries-old rules. Some of these ancient standards of measurement are so conservative and archaic that they can be overlooked with an easy conscience. Other standards arise from considerations so basic and sensible that they are still to be usefully employed.

Roots
Exposed roots across the surface of the soil suggest great age in a bonsai. If possible, these should be thick and vigorous, extending outward in all directions.

Trunk
The growth pattern and thickness of the tree's trunk have the greatest impact on its overall appearance. It should be especially thick at the base, gradually tapering toward the crown. Its entire form should characterize an old tree grown in the wild—yet have the harmony and distinction of a specimen plant.

Japanese maple *(Acer palmatum),* approximately 15 years old, growing in a round ceramic pot, 9½ inches (24 cm). Total height is 14 inches (35 cm).

Origins and Fundamentals

Bark
In certain trees, the bark of the trunk and the branches takes only a few years to attain the gnarls and knots of apparent great age. Other deciduous trees are prized for especially fine and evenly textured bark.

Limbs and Branches
Each bonsai has a "good side" from which its branches, trunk, and leafy crown are viewed to best advantage. Thus, the strongest, longest branches should grow to the right and left of this vantage point, while the smaller, thinner ones should fill out the back and front sides. In many cases growers let a few long branches grow toward the back to give the impression of great density. A bonsai needs a great variety of boughs and branches on a framework of harmoniously ordered and well-spaced larger limbs.

Foliage
Needles and leaves should basically be thick, with a healthy, vigorous color. Of course, plants with naturally small leaves are preferred.

Moss
In time, without any outside help, the surface of the earth around the bonsai will acquire a carpet of moss, giving the appearance of a carpet of lawn. Naturally, the moss should be finely textured and thick.

Pots
In size, form, color, and surface structure, the bonsai container should be chosen especially for the plant that will grow in it.

Every one of the points mentioned above is derived from a careful observation of nature. Follow these rules, acquire some practical expertise, and let your artistic sense be your guide. The end product will be the creation of a harmonious and stately bonsai.

Origins and Fundamentals

Bonsai Versus Natural Trees

In styling, a dedicated bonsai gardener has to observe and re-create even the smallest details. The gardener must use his or her skill to re-create the most exacting representation of nature, never forgetting that a finished bonsai overemphasizes the characteristics of a particular type of tree (or shrub). Very seldom indeed does a single tree in the wild possess all of the distinguishing familial characteristics. A bonsai incorporates the physical traits of an entire race of trees and exhibits them in their most concentrated form.

Bonsai concentrate years as well as traits, often making true age very difficult to ascertain. A very young tree can have the appearance of a similar but very much older wild tree if it has a relatively thick trunk and a bushy crown. Thus bonsai, a living work of art, has two ages—its own physical age and that of the tree it seeks to represent.

How Long Does a Bonsai Take?

When you see a bonsai for sale, it is at least 4 or 5 years old. Its underlying form has been developed and it can be considered fully finished. At this point it has undergone a whole series of culturing practices: Someone has undertaken the complicated and risky process of its propagation; it has been bred, improved, and regularly pruned and repotted; finally, the most artistic part of the work has been attempted—the training of its form.

Maintenance

The amount of care needed to maintain a bonsai in good health appears relatively minimal: Water every 2 days; cut back once or twice each year; fertilize once or twice a year; repot, root, and prune every 2 to 4 years. In addition, some trees need an annual re-wiring.

Thus the basic maintenance is relatively undemanding. Nevertheless, a bonsai's beauty and value grow steadily in direct proportion to the time devoted to it. Take a little time with your tree on a regular basis, follow the ripening of the leaf buds in spring, and you won't miss the first signs of life—the first tender leaves after a long winter. If you gradually mold the tree's crown, branches, and trunk into the shape that most appeals to you, you will experience a special pride when the crown of tiny leaves presents its display of color in the fall.

Origins and Fundamentals

An Inspiration—A Diary

Start a little diary for your bonsai in which you record all significant dates and events, all sicknesses and culturing practices—with dates written in and everything eventually augmented by photographs. In time you will have in your possession an impressive document, the chronicle of your bonsai. Perhaps your grandchildren and great-grandchildren will one day thank you on the occasion of the ceremonial presentation of the family bonsai—an old tradition in Japan.

Plants That Lend Themselves to Bonsai

Basically, almost all of the higher plants may be cultivated using the bonsai practice of restricting normal root development by using a small pot. Sooner or later, growth will diminish, leaves will stay smaller.

Stipulations

In actuality only a few plants have all of the characteristics necessary for a truly successful bonsai. The ideal bonsai plant should have a trunk capable of growing thick and woody in a short time. Its leaves or needles should be naturally small enough to be convincing. The roots should be clearly visible and capable of major surface growth.

They cannot be extraordinarily sensitive to regular, structural pruning.

Dwarf Growing Plants

Seasonal blooms or fruits should not be so large that they detract from the total appearance of the bonsai.

A natural diminishing in plant size—similar to that of the leaves—occurs when it is grown in a small flat pot. Nevertheless, when choosing a plant, preference should be given to the dwarf forms of a particular family.

Juniper (*Juniperus rigida*), approximately 45 years old. Ceramic container, 18×21 inches (53×36 cm). Total height, 44 inches (110 cm).

Origins and Fundamentals

Important: The most potentially successful bonsai plants don't have to be dwarf forms. The reverse is true as well: All dwarf forms are not necessarily suited to bonsai culture.

As we have already indicated, bonsai underwent its initial development in Japan, and it is naturally there that we find the plants traditionally used in bonsai culture. These plants are the ones commonly found in the Japanese landscape—natural vegetation with a firm place in the culture and mythology of Japan.

Favorite Bonsai Plants

(Details on page 48.)

Conifers
Chinese juniper, *Juniperus chinensi*
Japanese black pine, *Pinus thunbergii*
Japanese white pine, *Pinus parviflors, P. parvifora pentaphylla*

Deciduous Trees
Buerger's maple, *Acer buergerianum*
Japanese beeches, *Fagus* and *Caroinus*
Japanese maple, *Acer palmatum*
Japanese zelkova, *Zelkova*

Flowering and Fruit-Bearing Plants
Azaleas, *Azalea japonica*
Firethorn, *Pyracantha angustifolia*
Japanese flowering cherry, *Prunus donarium*
Rockspray, *Cotoneaster horizontalis*

Certainly there is a great number of native plants as suitable for bonsai as the traditional ones. The only thing missing is experience, for example, in such tasks as putting together the right soil mixture.

Of the 40,000 plants native to Japan, about 40 percent are woody plants, of which 80 percent are suitable for bonsai. Although Japan enjoys special botanical wealth due to its climate, even places less richly endowed may hope for a meaningful development of the bonsai hobby.

Care and Cultivation

Collecting in the Wild

The earliest history of bonsai was concerned essentially with plants found in nature that were potted and further trained. This method is perhaps the most promising; surely many of the most beautiful and famous old bonsai were created this way.

Plants already mature and re-sembling bonsai both in form and size are dug out of the ground with a sufficiently large root ball and then put in a pot. The best place to find such "stunted individuals" in nature is in mountainous areas with stony ground—where plants have only hollows or crevices to set down their roots, where storm and wind hurl microscopic particles of sand and ice that file away at the tender leaf buds, and where the tips of tender shoots are grazed off.

Follow a Schedule

Once you have found a promising plant, the work begins. Mark the exact spot in which your "super-plant" is to be found again. Next, contact the owner of the property to ask for permission to dig out and take the plant. Perhaps you can positively influence his decision by promising to plant another young nursery-grown plant in the same spot.

Although there are differences among types of plants, generally the best time to transplant is in the spring, when the leaf buds are still small and undeveloped. At this time, plants still haven't developed any new roots and the existing ones are dormant. The tree will be able to completely recover in the weeks that follow.

How to Dig Up a Tree

Next, remove all grass from around the trunk. Then look at the habit of the tree and trim or prune off all branches that are too long or un-necessary. Never, *never* employ brute strength, and simply grab the tree by the trunk to pull it out. Such action would damage the trunk, rip the roots, and shake off their life-giving soil. The best thing to do is to draw a circle around the trunk, half the width of the crown in diameter. This measurement is only approximate.

If the trunk is especially thick and the roots are quite strong, the diameter must extend even further. Shovel out a little ditch along this line. Roots you come across should be cut with a knife or a sharp clippers. When the ditch is half as deep as the diameter, slow-ly work toward the middle. Finally cut the thick taproot. Now the tree may be removed. All roots, sticking out of the root ball, should be

Care and Cultivation

In transplanting, a generous hole is dug around the root ball.

small pebbles to ensure good drainage. The soil of the root ball should be firmly pressed into the pot and thoroughly watered.

Subsequent Care
In the following weeks the plant must be sheltered from strong sun and wind, or root growth will be weakened. Spray the existing needles or leaves several times daily with water.

It usually takes about a month until the plant shows signs of life again. When it does, the trans-planting may be considered suc-cessfully completed. The occa-sional new shoot can be shortened with the fingers just behind the second or third leaf to encourage denser and finer branching. Put the tree in the sun gradually, at first only in the mornings and the late afternoons. A light fertilizing is also advantageous. In the fall, the con-dition of this future bonsai will be nearly normal. Although you will have to give it extra protection from wind and frost throughout the first winter, the following spring is the right time to take the first steps

cleanly cut away. Wrap the ball in newspaper and cover the whole thing snugly with plastic wrap bound together around the trunk.

Potting
The plant is greatly weakened by transplanting and must be potted as soon as possible. When un-wrapping the plant, it is absolutely mandatory to make sure that the ball doesn't fall apart. The strongest roots should now be cut diagonally once again. Now, the lit-tle tree can be situated in a pro-tected place in the garden or trans-planted into a deep pot with a hole for water runoff. The soil in the low-er third of the pot must allow water through easily. The layer on top of it should be finer and mixed with

toward dwarfing of the root ball. Repeat root pruning annually, until the ball is finally only a third or a half of the tree's crown in size.

Nursery Plants

Of course you can obtain the necessary raw material for bonsai cultivation in the nursery. Several dwarf false cypress, for example, grow unbelievably treelike and have long been used in bonsai culture. With luck, you will find among a hundred examples a tree with an especially thick trunk.

Quick Bonsai

The main problem with most nursery-grown plants is that the thickness of the trunk has no useful relationship to the height of the little tree. The impatient can still create a really attractive bonsai out of the raw material in a nursery by simply sawing off the trunk a hand's width above the soil surface. Radical root pruning should be done at the same time.

Like transplanting, care and cultivation must take place before the first shoots appear—at the latest in April. Below the cut new shoots will appear within a few weeks. These can be pinched as soon as they appear so later they will branch out and gradually form a crown. In summer, paint the cut on the little yard-high tree and give it some shelter. In winter such bonsai are not particularly attractive because the trunk and the branches have no harmonious relationship. Not until several years have passed will the cut be grown over enough so that only the practiced eye of an expert can guess the origin of the bonsai.

Trident maple *(Acer buergerianum),* approximately 15 years old, a year after it was radically cut back.

Care and Cultivation

The majority of moderately priced deciduous trees are produced by this method. More time-consuming methods drive the sales price up.

An Improved Method

A similar but not quite so radical method is often used in commercial bonsai production. Here, too, you select an older, larger plant with a few branches close to the earth. Saw through the trunk of the little tree right above the largest of the lower branches. A part of that branch will now become an extension of the trunk. If the scar between the two is too noticeable, technical means are used within the year to correct its growth. More about this technique will follow.

There is always the possibility of using the same "trick" on the same branch a little higher up—to cut the same branch back again and force another branch to take up the role of "leader." When this is done repeatedly, branches on alternate sides of the tree should be used as the new leaders. In that way the tree's natural symmetry will be restored and the trunk will wind up in a light zigzag movement. However, 2 cuts on the same side will weight the tree to that side; it is then very easily trained into a cascade form.

Root pruning will probably be necessary at this time and can be undertaken when you make the cuts.

Potting time is the right moment to make sure your tree has the proper balance—its dynamic form notwithstanding.

Time-saving methods like these allow bonsai nurseries to satisfy the need for thickly trunked but relatively inexpensive bonsai.

Care and Cultivation

Bonsai from Seed

Naturally, Bonsai can be raised from seed. This method is in the long run perhaps the most promising of all. Bonsai grown from seed can be trained into their given styles from the very first days of life. Later on—in most cases—these trees are simply qualitatively better. From a commercial viewpoint, the negative aspects of seed culture are the large expenditures of work and time. For the amateur grower they are the rather complicated requirements of seedlings. Many sections of the country lack the heat and humidity so beneficial to starting seeds without access to a greenhouse.

Seeding

In order to really take advantage of the summer growing season, the best time to sow seeds is in March or April.

Some types of trees, specifically conifers, need cold to break dormancy; it is best to keep the seeds in the refrigerator for a month or so. This is called "stratifying." On the day before the actual sowing, soak all of the seeds in a container of water. You can identify the good seeds at once. They are the ones not floating on the surface of the water. For the others, soaking will act to considerably shorten the germination time.

Use a deep dish or wooden box for a growing container. It should have an adequate drainage hole fitted with a little piece of screening to guard against its plugging up. To improve drainage, the bottom layer should be a layer of fine gravel; on top of that place a layer of soil about 4 inches (10 cm) thick, composed of equal parts of humus, sand loaf, and peat. Sow the seeds a few inches apart from each other and cover the whole thing with a finger-thick layer of earth.

Further Care

Germination can be accelerated by warmth. Place the planted seeds in a sunny, airy place. As soon as the seedlings appear, protect them from strong sunlight. Deciduous trees can take 2 months, conifers 3. Frequent misting and regular watering are important chores for good growth. July and August are the times to fertilize carefully for the first time. Protect the plants from frost without fail throughout the first winter. Examine the young plants regularly for pests, and if you must, spray the correct material in very weak concentration. After 2 or 3 years take the most robust seedlings out of the container and place them in pots for subsequent bonsai culture. These plants may or may not be the tallest ones.

Care and Cultivation

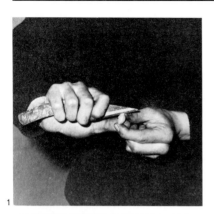

1. Seeds with hard coats *(gingko)* should be cut all around.
2. Leave enough room between the seeds.
3. Use a little trowel to cover the seeds with a finger-thick layer of soil.
4. 1- to 3-year-old spruces.

Care and Cultivation

Bonsai from Cuttings

Propagating certain trees this way is advantageous because the products are ready to use quickly and possess all of the desirable characteristics of the mother plant—something that cannot be guaranteed when seeding new plants. With seed, the genetic pool may turn up some undesirable traits, for example, a lessened bloom capacity or simply larger leaves.

Planting Cuttings

Prepare for planting cuttings the same way as you would for starting from seed. The only difference in materials is a higher proportion of sand in the soil mix. Early spring is the best time to propagate from cuttings. Look for the most robust branch—one with many leaves and leaf buds—and cut 2-inch-long (5–6 cm) tips off the branches. Make the cuts diagonally directly under leaf nodes. Insert half of their length into the soil.

Take care that no leaves are buried by soil because they will quickly rot and endanger the other cuttings. Spray the entire pot or box of new cuttings with water immediately after planting. Repeat several times each day.

1. Suckers from an azalea are being taken as cuttings.
2. The prepared cuttings in the soil mix.

Care and Cultivation

The first weak fertilizing should be done the following fall. By that time, the little shoots will have developed significantly. Thin out markedly puny or rotting plants.

The following spring, carefully remove the plants, placing each in its own 4-inch (10 cm) pot. Once the cuttings have established roots, they are indistinguishable from seedlings.

Proceed from here the same as with seedlings. The plants are allowed to grow unhindered for a few years in relatively large pots. Thereafter, they are placed in genuine, flat bonsai pots, limiting root growth, until the tree begins to acquire a bonsai's unique stature. Then the finer points of styling are carried out. The foliage of the tree should be trimmed at regular intervals, gradually forming a particular style.

1. Taking cuttings from a Chinese juniper.
2. A dish of cuttings.

Further Maintenance

The new cuttings should be protected from wind and very gradually accustomed to the sun. Take a week or so to acclimatize them. When there are frost warnings, bring the plants indoors, but otherwise don't hesitate to let them enjoy the refreshing dew.

Right: A Chinese juniper (Juniperus chinensis), approximately 12 years old. Glazed bowl, 10 inches (22 cm). Height, 22 inches (55 cm).

Care and Cultivation

Bonsai from Grafts

Propagation of bonsai from seeds or cuttings will produce excellent results. For the commercial grower, however, this approach requires an investment of too much work and time. Fortunately, the desired results can be brought about quickly using fast-growing woody plants. Using them as grafting stock provides a speedy alternative to the slower methods.

Grafting is accomplished by taking a scion (either a small rootless branch or a small shoot) of a rare and slow-growing plant and binding it to a fast-growing stock (a rooted but topless plant). The two grow as a single plant, exhibiting all of the desirable characteristics of the rare plant with some of the positive qualities of the root stock, such as quick growth.

An example of a successful graft is the union of the Japanese white and black pines. Japanese white pine, a traditional symbol of that country's landscape, is one of the most beloved bonsai plants. However, it grows so slowly that it takes more than a decade to produce an 8-inch-high (20 cm) bonsai. These slowly grown, ungrafted specimens are simply not to be found for sale here. In Japan a single plant can cost a small fortune.

Any white pine bonsai available here have been grafted to root-stock of the Japanese black pine (*Pinus thunbergii*). Japanese black pine brings its desirable attributes of fast growth and roots that tolerate pruning to the union.

Grafting Scars

The scar left by a graft is a clearly noticeable thickening of the trunk slightly above the soil. The more carefully and skillfully the grafting process is undertaken, the less noticeable the scar will be.

In time, the scar will fade but never really disappear for the simple reason that the barks of the Japanese black and white pines become more distinctive with age. The portion below the graft will be reddish brown and rough in texture, looking older than the relatively fine bark of the scion. Some bonsai styles allow for a grafting scar to be well concealed by branches. Many other conifers and deciduous trees are candidates for grafting. Another good combination is the false cypress and the Japanese maple.

Grafting possibilities are as numerous as they are complicated. To learn how to graft, you'd need a whole book's worth of information, if there is nobody around to demonstrate the use of a sharp grafting knife. This book will deal not so much with the process of grafting as the explanation of its why's and wherefore's.

Japanese peach, approximately 7 years old. The white blooming branch was grafted on about 2 years ago. Hexagonal ceramic pot, 5½ inches (14 cm) wide. Total height, 16 inches (40 cm).

Care and Cultivation

Bonsai from Air-Layering

The process of air-layering bonsai is simple: The upper section of a tree or its branches can be skillfully removed and made to grow as a bonsai. It can be used on almost all woody plants and gives relatively quick results. One particularly interesting result of this process is the formation of a tiny bonsai forest from particularly vigorous and well-shaped branches. However, this phenomenon has no commercial value because of its rare occurrence.

The following is a clear and concise guide to air-layering. There are two methods of air-layering. With the first method, a piece of bark approximately 1½ inches wide is cleanly removed with a sharp knife all around the tree. Where the bark is removed is where future roots will grow. With the second, a copper wire is wound so tightly around the trunk that it digs halfway into the tree. In both cases, the place where the bark has been severed is wound with moist spaghnum and covered with plastic, and then tied tightly around the lower end but loosely enough at the top to allow for watering. At this time all unnecessary branches should be removed. They will otherwise drain

1. The illustrations show the bark removed, and
2. The wire-binding of the bark.
3. Afterward, the spot is wrapped with spaghnum and plastic.

1   2   3

Care and Cultivation

strength from the weakened tree.

If these first steps are undertaken in early summer, it will take until fall for roots to form in the case of deciduous trees. A conifer may not grow roots until the following summer.

How long it takes for roots to form is largely dependent upon both air temperature and humidity. Spray the plants several times daily and shield them from direct sunlight in the weeks immediately following the air-layering. Whether or not it has been successful is usually evident within 10 to 14 days.

If the root system isn't adequately developed by fall, the removal of the top half will have to wait until the following year. For the best results, don't allow the tree to freeze—or, at least, protect its sensitive roots.

Finally, the trunk can be severed, and the upper part carefully planted. It is best to leave a part of the spaghnum around the roots to protect them. Keep the tree in half-shade and spray frequently for several weeks. Eventually it can be fertilized with a weak solution and kept in full sun.

After a year, the remaining spaghnum can be completely removed and the tree placed in a suitable container.

Bonsai Containers

Bonsai pots have 2 important functions. First, their small size is responsible for the characteristic dwarfed growth of the plants. Second, their appearance should be a visible complement and foundation for the tree growing within.

Generally, less expensive bonsai are sold in simple, round pots. These are mass-produced, machine-made articles used for importing. They do not jack up the price of the bonsai. They are practical—but in the long run are to be regarded as provisional because they have not been especially selected for the plant.

Every large city has at least one bonsai dealer who stocks a selection of more suitable bonsai containers in a variety of sizes. You will probably find both glazed and unglazed, round, oval, rectangular, very flat, and very high pots. Be sure to bring along your bonsai when you go to purchase a container. The best choice will be one that doesn't overwhelm the plant, but complements its size, color, shape, and texture; keep your eye on the plant and try to picture how it will look in any given pot. Colored or even highly glazed containers may sometimes work with a blooming or fruit-bearing tree. In any case, glazed containers keep the root ball moist longer and are

Care and Cultivation

Different bonsai containers.

not recommended for older conifers, which are particularly susceptible to fungi.

In choosing a pot style, carefully consider whether it complements the style of the plant. A strongly upright style without curves looks best in a simple rectangular container. A cascading form needs ballast—a larger, heavier pot. Last and most important, every bonsai container needs one or more adequately sized drainage holes.

Soil and Soil Mixtures

Soil, as has been mentioned, is an important factor in bonsai culture.

Basically, every kind of tree requires the type of soil found in its natural habitat. Over millennia, plants have evolved to suit their environments. Next to climactic factors, soil composition plays a decisive role. Because the correct soil isn't always available to the bonsai grower, one must combine various components to obtain it, adjusting the proportions to suit the needs of a particular plant.

Special Attributes of Bonsai Soils

Soils for bonsai have to be clean and as free from manure and com-

Care and Cultivation

A sieve with interchangeable parts and the traditional Japanese watering can.

post as possible, since fertilizing is done artificially in order to promote regular but limited growth. In addition, before mixing and potting, the substratum should be crumbly and loose, composed of different-sized soil particles to ensure better drainage and air supply in the pot.

Specialty stores in Japan carry a wide variety of soils from all the different areas of the country. However, for most purposes, 3 basic soil types will do; namely: coarse sand, loam, and humus.

Optimum Proportions

Conifers:
50 percent loam and 50 percent sand, or, depending upon age, up to 100 percent loam.

Deciduous trees:
60 percent loam, 30 percent sand, 10 percent humus.

Flowering and fruiting plants:
50 percent loam, 30 percent sand, 20 percent humus.

For those who wish to follow traditional methods precisely, the container must be filled with 3 different sizes of earth particles obtained by screening through different-sized sieves. Bonsai specialty stores carry sieves with mesh sizes from ⅓ to ¹⁄₁₆ inch (3 to 1 cm) holes. The ⅓ inch size allows through coarse particles, even small pebbles, to form the bottom layer in the pot. The middle layer consists of slightly smaller-sized particles, while fine soil makes up the rest. Particles that are too fine and may later filter down into the pot to clog and diminish good drainage are sieved out so that all-important air spaces and drainage are preserved.

Care and Cultivation

Potting and Repotting

After a bonsai has been in a pot for several years, the pot is likely to be filled with roots. At some point, these will become so crowded that they will begin to rot. But even before that happens, the soil will have become so worn out that it requires replacement. Exactly when this occurs depends upon the type of tree, its age, the pot size, and the composition of the soil mixture.

It is best to take a good look at the root ball at least twice each year and postpone potting until the roots have formed a clearly visible tight net of roots around it.

The best time of year to prune the roots is nearly always in the months of March and April, before new growth begins; with a few conifers, fall is recommended. Later in this book, specific dates will be listed.

Important Preparations
In order for repotting to proceed smoothly so that the unprotected root system need not suffer unduly, it is recommended that all the necessary tools and materials are laid out, ready to use. If a new pot is being used, the drainage hole should be fitted with a bit of screening to prevent soil from slipping out.

Besides prepared, thoroughly dried soil, you will need the following:

- A small trowel.
- A very sharp, clean shears.
- A flat or rounded wooden stick.
- A spray bottle of water.

When the bonsai is repotted, it should have gone long enough without watering to be almost dry; that way, the soil will be lighter and easier to remove from the roots.

Care and Cultivation

Procedure

Find a shady place out of the wind to work. Grasp the bonsai by the trunk and try to lift it out of its pot. Some containers have an inward curving rim that makes this practically impossible. In that case, use the wooden stick to loosen the upper surface of the soil and roots until the tree slips out comfortably.

Lay the bonsai on its side after taking it out of the pot. Grasping its trunk firmly with one hand, carefully and thoroughly loosen the roots with a wooden stick until they hang freely.

Younger trees may have about half of the root ball removed, older trees somewhat less. Use clean cuts to remove most of the loose hanging roots; the thick taproot may only be cut on a clean diagonal.

1. White fungus growth on the side of this unpotted ball is clearly visible. It is a sign of healthy growth. 2. and 3. From top to bottom, the roots are carefully unraveled.

Care and Cultivation

4. Cut the root ball in this manner.
5. Sever the taproot with a diagonal cut.

place for the plant, especially when its shape is asymmetric. For balance, of course, the tree's foliage should be wider than the pot on all sides.

Place the trunk slightly off center to one side or to the back. Now spread out the roots carefully in all directions around the trunk, filling in gradually with the medium-fine soil. The little wooden stick will help to fill in the hard-to-reach spaces. Sprinkle the finest soil to fill in the top fifth.

For better visual integration of plant and container, make sure that the top of the soil reaches the rim of the pot, mounding slightly to meet the trunk. The bonsai should stand in its designated place without wobbling. Freshly added soil may be lightly pressed in, and if necessary the stability of the tree can be ensured in the first weeks by wrapping a cord snugly around the exposed roots, and finally around the whole pot.

Finally, spray the base of the trunk and any surface roots that may have been covered by soil clean, using a spray bottle of water. Use your hand (or even better, a brush) to flatten the top surface of the soil. Then give the bonsai a thorough watering.

Now the actual repotting can begin. Fill the pot one-fifth full of the coarsest soil. Or substitute a mixture of a little crumbly soil and pebbles for better drainage. After placing a thin layer of middle-grade soil in the pot, position the plant on it. The exact center of the container isn't necessarily always the right

6.–10. Preparations for potting and actual procedure. (See page 34.)

11. The top of the earth surface is smoothed.

12. Roots are exposed by using a spray bottle of water.

37

Care and Cultivation

Afterward

Shield freshly potted bonsai from both strong sunlight and wind for at least 2 to 4 weeks. Spray several times each day so that new feeder roots can develop. To avoid unnecessary transpiration, remove extra needles, branches, or leaves.

Watering

A bonsai is only watered when the top surface is dry. Take great care, however, not to wait so long between waterings that cracks develop in the surface. After a certain point, the soil will become so completely dry that it actually sheds water; if that happens, water will simply flow around the root ball without being absorbed by it. To remedy this situation, you'll have to water several times—one after another—until you observe that the soil is again absorbing water.

Sun and wind act as growth-hindering factors by drying out the earth faster, but they should never be allowed to actually wilt a plant. On hot summer days, a plant may require up to 3 waterings. In winter, when dormant, the same plant may require only 1 watering per week. Watering should never be only the soil, especially in summer; the whole tree benefits from a good shower. Naturally, do this in such a way that the soil doesn't wash away, in which case no moss will grow. A small, easy-to-handle watering can with a fine spray is best for this purpose.

When the tree is in full bloom, a good dousing is not recommended because it will quickly rot the colorful blossoms. Always water copiously so that water flows out of the drainage hole at the bottom of the pot.

Japanese white pine *(Pinus parviflora),* approximately 20 years old. Ceramic pot, 13½ × 10 inches (34 × 25 cm). Total height, 18 inches (45 cm).

Care and Cultivation

You may tend to under-water your bonsai in winter, especially if it is kept in the house and you are cautious about your carpets and windowsills. And placing a protective pot or cache-pot under the bonsai may raise the hair on a true bonsai-lover's neck. When you water, do it outside or in the bathtub.

Tap water does the job, but can be harmful to the plant in the long run. Remove any chalky substance you find on the surface roots with water and brush. In all cases, it is best to use rain water, or at the very least boiled water or water that has been allowed to stand.

Fertilizers

Bonsai can live for about a year without feeding before leaves and branches dry out, a fate that is hastened by small container size and a correspondingly small amount of earth whose reservoir of minerals are quickly spent. Plants growing in nature are able to use a wide-ranging root system to acquire the nourishment they need.

Understandably, there cannot be any general rule for feeding bonsai because every type, every single plant has its own special needs. The right dose depends on pot size, plant type, and soil composition.

Conifers, green year-round, need nourishment in winter, while feeding most deciduous trees in winter will cause root rot. A fertilizer generally should contain 3 main ingredients—nitrogen, phosphorus, and potassium—along with a number of trace elements often present in the bonsai soil. Blooming and fruit-bearing trees require greater percentages of phosphorus and potassium. (See page 80 for more detailed information.)

What Do You Use for Fertilizer
Commercially available fertilizer in liquid or powdered form may not be used as directed on the package label. Instead, always use it half-strength.

Substances traditionally used to manure bonsai are ashes, ground horn, oilcake, and, above all, rapeseed, which can be spread across the top of the soil where it will gradually dissolve. It may also be used in concentration with 20 to 30 pints of water. Specialty shops have recently begun carrying fertilizers with exactly the right composition for Japanese bonsai. These come in tablet form.

Care and Cultivation

4 pieces of fertilizer are anchored to the soil surface by wires.

Bonsai Aren't House-plants

This chapter is surely the most important in terms of maintenance because it is in the house that most of the greatest errors are made. Bonsai are not perpetual houseplants, but normal trees in miniature form. Tropical plants survive in our houses because they require warmth in winter. Japanese trees, like other trees in the northern hemisphere, have a need for a dormant period in winter "programmed" into their life cycles. Forced to stay in dry house heat, a tree will quickly become exhausted. It simply needs a rest period in its growth cycle.

The Right Location

Keep your bonsai outside, bringing it into a well-ventilated room in summer for a day or so. Eventually it may remain there for up to a few weeks. Most bonsai trees are absolutely winter-hardy. Nevertheless, they still require a little extra protection. First, the root ball in its small ceramic bowl is rather unprotected. Second, very thin branches can be simply "freeze dried" by the wind.

Place your tree in a wind-protected corner, cover the pot with cloth, newspaper, or turf, and insulate the bottom with Styrofoam.

Care and Cultivation

Deciduous trees are best stored in a bright, well-ventilated, frost-free room with a temperature no higher than 35 F (10 C) because their twigs and branches are easily cold-damaged. If you have no garden at your disposal in the winter, a staircase, a garage, or a basement window can serve very well. In spring, put the bonsai outside as soon as possible, bringing it in again on nights when frost threatens in order to protect any developing buds.

Diseases and Pests

A tree in a pot is just as vulnerable to disease and pests as those in the open. There is almost always a serious oversight in maintenance to blame when a plant loses its natural immunity. When the disease or pests are removed, it will only regain that immunity if the source of its weakness is not identified and treated.

Root Rot

One common cause of other pests is root rot, from which no species of tree is immune. Generally it is caused by an inappropriate soil composition, a stopped-up drainage hole, or too-frequent watering. In all cases, the bottom of the container becomes a swamp—good drainage and air spaces are eliminated. Sometimes the bonsai will have been too dry for some time, a condition that will kill tiny feeder roots. After they die, they begin to rot. Possibly the bonsai was repotted at the wrong time and overwatered. All of this, of course, sounds more complicated than it really is, but deserves to be mentioned here. If you don't know what is causing the trouble, you'll have to carefully remove the bonsai from its pot and examine the root ball. Sickness is clearly recognizable by dark brown, mushy roots. The best thing to do is to slice off all affected roots and replace the infected soil with fresh, clean earth.

For best results follow up with a disinfectant.

Crabapple *(Malus haliana)*, approximately 10 years old. Ceramic pot, 7×7 inches (17×17 cm). Total height, 19 inches (46 cm).

Care and Cultivation

Pests

Somewhat less common, aphids, woolly apple aphids, and cottony scale sometimes trouble bonsai—usually after they have been in the house for too long. The remedy is a commercially available spray—preferably thinned to one-quarter strength—and perhaps a preparation to soak the soil.

No matter whether sickness, pests, or an overlong stay in the house caused the initial weakening, first-aid measures must be taken immediately. The bonsai needs protection from sun, wind, and frost, and should be sprayed several times daily in order to prevent dessication.

Tools

For successful shaping, the few tools described in the following passages are highly recommended. You should select high-quality tools designed for specific purposes. Well-designed, valuable bonsai tools imported from Japan are available from specialty stores. Dull or even jagged knives and scissors are unusable and may inflict lasting damage.

You need the following:

- Clean, sharp shears of different sizes to clip leaves, twigs, and roots.

- A handy, fine-toothed saw for thick branches and roots.
- A sharp, short knife.
- Powerful clippers for cutting wire; narrow clippers with a long handle to make work in a thickly grown crown easier.
- Round-nosed flat clipper for winding wire.
- Pointed trowel or shovel.
- Wooden or bamboo sticks for all purposes.
- A wide brush for flattening the soil surface.
- A small, handy watering can with a fine spray.
- A powerful spray bottle for water, fertilizer, and applying insecticide; the spray should be fine and adjustable.
- Flexible annealed or anodized copper and aluminum wire for shaping.

Care and Cultivation

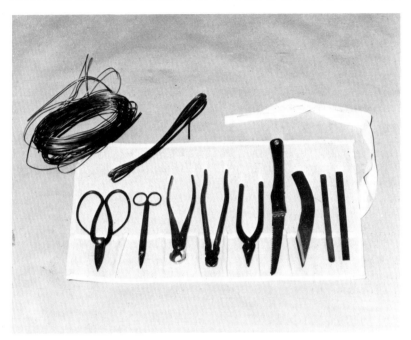

In the upper left of this photo is styling wire in different weights for trunk and branches. Then from left to right:

- Handy branch shears strong enough for thicker branches.
- A somewhat lighter version with extra-long handles for working in hard-to-reach places in the crown and for snipping off buds. The bigger clipper can easily cut off small twigs.
- Powerful nippers for thick branches and roots. It has to be both steady and sharp. A dull, jagged nippers will inflict grave damage.
- Large wire clippers. This one has long handles for work among the branches and leaves of the crown. Extremely useful, it is used for removing thick wires from around the trunk which must be cut every inch or so.

- Small wire clippers for winding thin or medium-sized wire so securely that it doesn't slip and eventually damage bark.
- A fine pocket hand saw. In many cases, this is a better tool to use for thick roots and branches than the large branch clippers.
- Sharp, handy, and powerful knife to create the *jin* effect and to cut out ugly scars.
- Two different scalpels for air-layering, grafting, etc.

Styling

Goals and Reasons

A plant becomes a bonsai only after years of expert shaping give it both balance and style. Without the constant intervention of the bonsai gardener, small vigorous branches would quickly turn the bonsai into wild, stalky growth in all directions. Less vigorous branches might simply dry up. To become a future masterpiece, the bonsai requires enormous attention to styling. This process demands much more than a simple regular pruning of all branches. The original, fascinating essence of bonsai thought lies in eliciting from natural plant material a truly individual bonsai that looks as if it were shaped by environmental forces.

A good eye and a steady hand will develop quickly by observing both nature and good examples of bonsai as well as by effort. While fanciful and unusual styles are eye-catching, keep in mind that later on the overall appearance of your bonsai should express unity and harmony. Bonsai in Japan is a discipline with a long tradition. Very specific ground rules have been set down, stipulating in detail the procedures for shaping a number of possible bonsai styles, even dividing these styles into categories. For us, working with miniature trees is an interesting hobby without a long tradition of religious and philosophical thought behind it. Yet, this involvement with another culture enriches our lives.

Japanese white pine *(Pinus pentaphylla)*, approximately 35 years old. Ceramic pot, 16×11 inches (39×28 cm). Total height, 26 inches (65 cm).

Styling

Most Popular Bonsai Styles

The Formal Upright Style

is one of the most "natural." The trunk is perfectly straight. Because of the extreme simplicity of this style, total symmetry is to be avoided. Branches should alternate, left and right; to suggest age, branches along the bottom quarter of the trunk are removed and the remainder are drawn downward.

The Informal Upright Style

is characterized by a lightly curving trunk. In the wild, this kind of tree would have prevailed against the harsh forces of nature for decades and thus represents great vigor. For many amateurs this style is the most promising because it can be achieved with relative ease with wires or cords. It is as appropriate for conifer as it is for deciduous. Training branches into a clearly demarked stair-step arrangement lends a feeling of peace and stability to an otherwise lively, dynamic style.

Beech
Cypress
Elm
Fir
Japanese black pine
Japanese white pine
Juniper
Larch
Maple

Oak
Pine
Many deciduous trees

Styling

The Broom Style

has a straight trunk that begins to divide and subdivide into many branches at a given point. Characteristic is its thick and finely branched crown.

Beech
Elm
False cypress
Maple

The Slanting Style

depicts a tree with the kind of oblique attitude acquired in the wild by shifting in the earth's crust or severe storms. Branches should be absolutely horizontal.

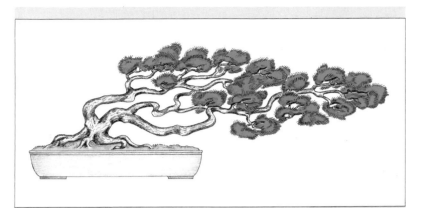

The Windblown Style
is rare. In nature, it is the kind of
tree found on cliffs or mountains
whose trunk, branches, and twigs
have been trained in a single direction by the strong and steady
action of wind and storm.

Azalea
Japanese white pine

Maple
Pine

51

Styling

The Clasped-to-Stone Style
is much loved but difficult to create. A tree, utterly exposed to and formed by the forces of nature, clings to an interesting rock, set on a dish of gravel or water. In some cases, roots may extend all the way down the rock wall into a pot of earth below. The size and shape of the stone should complement the plant. When training this style, care should be exercised that the stone isn't composed of salt-retaining minerals. If the rock doesn't already have holes, these will have to be chiseled out. A little piece of lead is useful in boring out discrete holes for hidden anchor wires and cords; these cords bind the roots to the stone until they establish their own holds.

False cypress
Juniper
Maple

Styling

The Double-Trunk Style
is formed when a single tree divides into 2 trunks right above the ground; these 2 sections must be harmoniously divided. Frequently, Japanese white pine is used for this style, because when it is young it is fairly easy to train a strong branch and the trunk into the desired shape.

The Clump Style
looks like a group of trees, but like the double-trunk style grows from a single root system. Often this style originates in skillful air-layering of the upper section of a tree.

Styling

Juniper
Maple
Pine
Spruce

Pine
Juniper
Spruce

Styling

The Raft Style

is a line of separate trunks all growing from a buried and rooted branch. Very rare.

Beech
Elm
Fir
Maple
Japanese white pine
Spruce

Forests

are a number of plants of different heights and thicknesses positioned into a harmonious group. For aesthetic reasons, the rule is for an uneven number.

Beech
Cypress
Elm
Maple
Pine

Styling

Styling

Cascades and Half-Cascades have to be imagined growing on mountains at the mercy of the elements, where they are forced into horizontal or hanging positions. Such bonsai look best with the visually stabilizing counterweight of a tall, rather narrow pot. For the Japanese, cascades express an emotional spectrum ranging from melancholy to deep sorrow—depending on how low the tree is bent.

Fruit tree
Ivy
Juniper
Pine
Willow

Styling

How Styles Are Trained

The techniques of shaping are as interesting for the person who wishes to train a young plant as for the one who has purchased a fully formed bonsai.

Determining the Basic Shape
Look at the plant very carefully before deciding which style is most suitable. To make a really fine specimen, attention to its development must be thorough and all-encompassing—down to the smallest detail.

Front and Back Sides
The attitude and constitution of the tree trunk, the length and spread of its branches, as well as its exposed roots, are all decisive attributes in ultimately choosing the style. The strongest branches on the right and left of the trunk should remain, but any really substantial growths toward the front will have to be removed. To give an impression of depth, branches growing toward the back side may be left in place.

Thinning
The next step is establishing an airy transparency in the foliage by thinning out unnecessary parts of the tree. Don't do too much of a good thing or the trunk may suddenly appear too powerful for the rest of the tree. Young plants generally don't need thinning and in old ones, it can sometimes cause an imbalance—especially if the trunk is already thick. A thick trunk must be counterbalanced by an adequate framework of branches.

The following branches should always be removed:

- 1 of 2 that parallel each other.

The red lines indicate where to cut.

Styling

- 1 of any 2 that cross (a correction is sometimes possible by wiring).
- All except 1 growing at the same height around the trunk (the so-called "wagon wheel effect").
- Any that grow across the trunk.
- Any that are growing from the bottom quarter of the trunk.

Removing branches may be accomplished with shears; thicker ones may require a saw. Watch that the bark of the tree is not unnecessarily damaged; in difficult cases, try to protect it by wrapping it with cloth or adhesive tape. After removing a branch, the remaining stump should be cut flush with the trunk. In older bonsai, a stump an inch long or even the fork of a tree can be artfully treated to give the impression of an old tree, struck by lightning, whose great limb has been broken off. The name given to this artistic scarring is *jin.* It can greatly enhance the apparent age of a bonsai.

After thinning the main scaffolding, the branches are next. In this process, avoid an oversymmetrical and repetitious appearance. Finally trim the foliage into several "stair steps," allowing no stray branch tips to poke out of the mass of foliage and ruin the overall effect. Although small, thin twigs may be pruned at any time of year, hold off cutting larger branches until winter when the tree is dormant.

Styling with Wire and Cord

Wrapping branches and boughs with wire is a modern technique for making selected plant material into attractive bonsai. Another interesting objective of this method might be the modeling of an already formed bonsai into another shape.

How Is It Done?
The principle couldn't be more simple: Different grades of wire wound around the pliable wood to hold the position into which it has been bent. After a year, in which time the desired shape will be fixed, you can remove the wire. Wiring is not, as is commonly thought, a means of stunting the plant's growth.

Styling

When Do You Wire?

The right season to wire is, in most cases, while the tree is dormant, between October and March. At this time wiring affects the tree least. Exceptions are some conifers, particularly the Japanese white pine, which should be handled in early summer, when the sap is running and the branches are easier to bend.

Which Wire Should Be Used?

Generally copper wire that has been fired for greater flexibility is recommended. Then it has the advantage of being very easy to bend. The disadvantage with copper is that its surface may attract galvanized elements that could damage the tree.

Iron wire rusts too fast and ruins the bark. Aluminum or zinc wires are too noticeable, spoiling the tree's appearance. The best of all is one especially made for bonsai, an anodized aluminum wire that can sometimes be obtained in bonsai hobby shops. Another alternative is plastic-coated florist's wire, manufactured in subtle colors. Because of its soft surface it is also unlikely to irritate the bark. The thinner the wire, the easier it is to work with; however, it still has to be strong enough to mold the tree.

Wiring Procedure

A bonsai should be wired from
bottom to top. Use a thick wire and
start by sinking one end between
the roots. Wind the other end
around the trunk in large diagonal
curves, taking care not to skin off
the bark. If one wire isn't strong
enough, another will have to be
wound parallel to the first. It is
far better to wire large curves in
several stages over months because if the tree cracks anywhere,
that part of the plant is as good as
dead. As a last resort you can try to
wrap the broken ends with raffia or
garden tape.

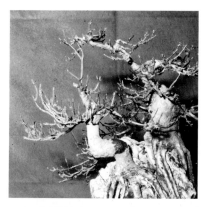

Raw material—in this case a Japanese
white pine—is wired into a clear, harmonious form.

Styling

The wiring of limbs and branches is similar to wiring the trunk; the chief difference is the use of various grades of thinner wire. When branches grow too closely together, cut off a piece double the length of the tree (rather too long, because if you have to patch the curves won't be smooth), the middle of which is wound around the trunk and then outward toward the branches.

A branch is brought into a better position to improve appearance.

Styling

Don't wind too loosely, but do take care not to dig into the bark. After you've spread the branches as far as is prudent, proceed (using thinner wire) to other, smaller branches that may be too close together, and so on.

Always wind the ends around the wood and cut them off. The wiring should be absolutely firm, with no loose ends to come undone. If a particular branch is too difficult to wire, it's better to leave it alone until later when your skills have improved.

After Wiring the Shape

Finally, the tree has been wired from top to bottom in the desired shape. The beauty of most conifers and many older deciduous trees is greatly enhanced by a gradual, stair-step arrangement of the branches from bottom to top. This phenomenon is observed in nature, with the tree's foliage growing in cloudlike billows of different shapes and sizes that are distinct from each other. Bonsai takes this natural occurrence and idealizes it. Wired limbs are pulled down toward the trunk. This positioning has a unifying effect on the small branches and twigs. They grow together forming a layer that billows up—and only up. Viewed from the front, the underside of these stair-stepping limbs will be flat.

There is a point worth mentioning regarding the styling process. Nearly all young, vigorous woody plants have limbs that grow straight up, while great old trees are adorned with drooping limbs. You work against nature in bonsai culture when you take a fast-growing limb and pull it down. If the tips of a large number of branches are being pulled down by wires, it takes too much energy from the tree. It's better to bend the very tips of the wired-down branches lightly back up. With pines, young shoots must point straight up.

Further Care

The rigors of the styling process will exhaust the tree and make protection from the sun and wind, and spraying the tree several times daily, a necessity. Avoid using fertilizer or insecticide at this time; repotting should be put off for several weeks as well. Likewise, freshly repotted bonsai shouldn't be immediately wired.

Removing the Wires

After a year (at the very latest), when the wire begins to dig into the bark of the tree, it will have to be removed. The process is the exact reverse of wiring. First, the finest, thinnest twigs are unwound, working slowly from the outside in.

Styling

The heaviest wire should be clipped every half-inch with a clippers; trying to unwind and pull it out will break the branches. Wire that has grown into the trunk requires the greatest care in removal, which can be done without grave consequences as long as it is only about half-buried. Beyond that point, it is better to simply let it grow into the tree. Although this solution leaves unpleasant and permanent scarring, the bonsai won't suffer any unusual damage. In nature, a tree like that would be broken off in a storm sooner or later.

If after the unwiring the tree still requires some correction, you'll have to rewire the part that needs it.

Using Cord to Train Bonsai

Some bonsai gardeners work with cords because they are easier on the tree trunk and not as unsightly while they are in use. Very thin string is excellent for smaller correction in the scaffolding; however, for bigger jobs wire works better.

Using cord takes longer than wire because while a single wire can be wound in every imaginable direction, cord is always strung between 2 points in 1 dimension so that many cords are necessary in order to create a given effect. With commercially produced bonsai, this effort drives the price up. Thus,

bonsai trained in this manner are rarely seen in trade. When they do occur, it is generally a tree trained in a dynamic "S" shape with many curving limbs that appear a bit abnormal but have nevertheless a certain appeal.

Shoot Pruning

This area of bonsai culture is as interesting as it is important. There are numerous reasons for pruning:

- Shortening the shoots hinders the growth of the entire plant.
- The tree sends out more branches and the foliage is thicker.
- Pruning stimulates the secondary growth buds that have smaller leaves and are altogether finer in appearance.
- Pruning furthers even growth overall, while it prevents 1 or 2 especially vigorous shoots from draining the tree's energy.
- Bonsai, whose chief attraction rests in the development of flowers or fruit, need pruning to induce bountiful blooming and fruit-bearing.

Styling

When and how pruning is undertaken depends on the type of tree. The following are procedures to follow for various kinds:

Japanese White Pine

produces new growth once each year. Remove unnecessary shoots, particularly when several are growing out of the same place. Likewise branches that are quite vigorous can be halved or slowed down

through the removal of their candles (as the shoots of needle evergreens are called). Remove the candles in early summer before they are more than 3 inches long, but not before they open.

Most Other Needle Evergreens

get new growth twice each year. In June, remove all vigorously growing candles with the fingernails or a shears. Some weeks later several

new buds will replace the ones you've removed—but they won't be as big. Let at least 2 or 3 of them fully develop; otherwise, you'll stunt the tree.

Firs, Spruces, and Junipers

New shoots have to be regularly shortened. The best way to do this is carefully with the fingernails or simply by twisting them off.

Styling

Maples, Elms, and Beeches

During the growing season, regularly cut back to the second or third leaf.

Flowering and Fruit-Bearing Plants

Cut most shoots back entirely, leaving only a selected few. Wait until fall to shorten rangey branches—but don't shorten too much, or there won't be good bloom in the following year.

Styling

The Leaf-Cutting Method

This method makes use of another interesting botanical phenomenon useful for bonsai purposes. It is standard treatment on all maples and elms to achieve finer and denser branching on thick trunks and limbs. An additional and desirable result of this method is the production of smaller leaves —though they won't appear until the following year.

Procedure

After they are fully developed, cut off all of the leaves with a sharp scissors, so that when you are done, only the stems are left. A few weeks later, these will begin to dry up and fall off. As far as your tree is concerned, you have produced an early fall. As a result, the tree will experience a second spring, in which the dormant leaf buds are stimulated into new leaves. As already mentioned, these won't be as big as the original leaves and— what is even more curious—much fine branching can be achieved in a single summer. In very mild climates, like Japan, the leaf-cutting method can be used over and over again within a single year.

Important

A bonsai that has been leaf-trimmed must be protected from hot sun and strong wind for several weeks and should be sprayed several times each day. A liquid fertilizer applied before and after the trimming will help to carry the plant through this unaccustomed stress.

Use the leaf-cutting method only on healthy bonsai—never shortly after repotting or wiring. Weaker limbs are handled gingerly, in that they needn't have the entire leaf cut away but only a half.

69

Purchased or Home-Grown

At this point you have been exposed to basically everything worth knowing about the care, the background, and the styling of a bonsai. You may have even formed some of your own ideas about the possibility of creating a living work of art using your own imagination and skill—all the while discovering much about the natural beauty of plants.

The demands made on the gardener interested in bonsai, namely the development of special new gardening capabilities—such as a certain aesthetic sense—constitute both the challenge and the special attraction of bonsai. To many the artistic aspect is most appealing, while others are fascinated by the botanical side of bonsai. Shall I buy a bonsai—or should I try to create my own?

Japanese maple *(Acer palmatum)*, approximately 20 years old. Oval ceramic bowl, 13×9 inches (32×23 cm). Total height, 35 inches (71 cm).

In either case, the first bonsai shouldn't be too valuable or too complicated. Every beginner makes a few mistakes and these can have devastating effects on the health of the little tree. One of these is the well-meaning bringing inside of the plant when it rains or is cold outside.

The Purchased, Finished Bonsai

It has certain advantages:

- You can concentrate totally on care alone and eventually learn its needs; for example, how much water is just right.
- Using your tree as an example, you can learn something about correct wiring and shaping by intense observation.
- You will avoid possible disappointment if your own efforts go wrong, the other possibility.

Nevertheless, you shouldn't be afraid one day to take on your own bonsai. Your relationship to it will eventually develop into a deep one. True individualists among bonsai lovers will certainly never be satisfied with ready-made trees and sooner or later will begin their own with reasonable success.

Purchased or Home-Grown

Gather information about the growth habits of native flora on walks in mountain forests. Perhaps you'll find an extraordinarily interesting tree, which can serve as a model—or even as raw material—for your own bonsai. Visit a good nursery and be on the lookout for appropriate plants. Especially promising are some of the false cypresses *(Chamaecyparis obtusa nana gracilis),* beeches, and birches, as well as many azaleas. Find the largest possible selection to seek out the one little tree that meets the following criteria:

- Thick trunk.
- Bushy foliage.
- Small and subtle grafting scar.

Trees taken directly from the ground have to be potted as quickly as possible and may possibly need some root and branch pruning. The best time of year to do this is spring.

Bonsai for the Home

Traditional bonsai in Japan have used the flora of that country's temperate climate for raw material. You can be a pioneer and select the flora from other regions. Look among subtropical, or even better, tropical plants that have a thick trunk and small leaves. I have personally achieved success with ten-

der azaleas, camellias, *Ficus benjamina,* and myrtle. A most unusual bonsai plant is a palm fern *(Cycas revoluta),* called a sago palm, which can live inside without a problem.

Azalea *(Azalea japonica),* around 20 years old. Oval ceramic dish, 16×12 inches (40×30 cm). Height, 18 inches (45 cm).

Purchased or Home-Grown

How Much Should a Bonsai Cost?

Prices of plants found in the trade are determined by the amount of work expended in the creation of the bonsai and indirectly to the age of the plant. Deciduous trees require more work than conifers due to their need for constant pruning. Naturally, quality plays a role, too, although not particularly in the case of very young bonsai destined for the market in a few years. The second price-determining factor is transport cost, which represents a larger percentage of the cost of cheaper bonsai than it does for real showpieces.

A few years ago, quarantine regulations for bonsai with root balls were very strict, but today importing is somewhat easier. Then, the law stating that a plant had to remain in the greenhouse of the importer a full year (thereby incurring immense expense) could be gotten around by simply washing off the earth of the root ball. Officials had no reason to detain them and they entered the country *en masse.* Once they arrived, they needed pots that, depending upon their quality, added once again to the price. And of course, the dealers wanted to earn their profit, because a bonsai will often be tied up capital, sitting in the shop for a long time—not quickly sold like an ordinary pot of flowers. Even so, you can still find inexpensive bonsai. If you are prepared to spend more, you will acquire a more attractive tree. And you'll almost always fare relatively better with an older, more expensive tree.

Bonsai as Investments?

Anything you pay for a bonsai is money out the window if you don't first understand the basics of watering and the plant dies. Bonsai gain slowly and steadily in value.

On one side is the real worth, determined by age, quality, and the beauty of the tree. Unlike an ordinary work of art, a bonsai improves aesthetically as it ages. That isn't the only reason for the constant rise in value. In the West, bonsai has finally attained a permanent niche; confidence in importation as a long-lasting development rather than a passing trend has been underscored by voluminous investments. And if the market eventually develops throughout the world, the supply of old bonsai in Japan will dry up. Before long the export of really top-quality pieces will stop. In the foreseeable future, then, medium-priced plants too will become scarce, an event that will be heralded by ridiculously high prices. Therefore, good bonsai are to be seen as thoroughly promising investments. Beyond the real value of a bonsai is its ideal value.

Purchased or Home-Grown

When the relationship of owner to tree is laced with many stories and experiences, one scarcely thinks about material worth. Such has been the case in Japan for centuries.

Where and How to Buy

If beauty and quality mean something to you, don't buy the first good bonsai you see.

The Bonsai Season Begins in Winter

Probably you'll choose your plant from the large number available in the winter months, when the transport ships come from Japan. Bonsai are packed like sardines into crates and wrapped in moist spaghnum moss. They aren't watered once for the entire six weeks the trip takes, which seems incredible. This is possible only because the plants are kept at a temperature slightly above freezing, 35 F (4 C). The best time to buy is in winter.

Bonsai Specialty Shops

Even if they are available cheaply in garden centers and supermarkets, to be on the safe side, choose the specialty shop. There you can get advice. Later you can also buy fertilizer, soil, pots and dishes, and genuine Japanese tools—all especially made for bonsai culture. No dealer in the whole world can give you an unconditional guarantee for a bonsai, simply because it is a living being, and once it is sold, becomes the responsibility of the new owners. However, the seller has a duty to give you information regarding the difference between the care of bonsai and that of normal potted plants. Especially important is the fact that expensive bonsai don't belong inside for any length of time.

It is up to you when buying a tree, to take a good look at its conditions and check if:

- The bonsai is firmly rooted and doesn't wobble in its pot. If it moves around, either there's something wrong with the root system or it was only recently imported and potted—in which case, although the tree isn't sick, it is weak and needs tender loving care for a while. If you have the choice, it's better to leave a plant like this alone.

Purchased or Home-Grown

- The foliage has to be fresh and green. Spots on the leaves could possibly indicate either pests or sickness. Pine needles mustn't be dry or strawlike.
- Be on the lookout for brittle branches and dried-out twigs.

Trees that have been potted for some time and have a firm root ball can be carefully lifted out of their pots. If you are genuinely interested in purchasing a given tree, in most cases, the seller will gladly unpot the tree in your presence to let you check the condition of the roots. They shouldn't be dark brown or mushy, a sure sign of root rot. Bad bonsai are rarely found in bonsai nurseries. But it's always better to check first.

Japanese zelkova—the same example without and with foliage. (See also page 94.)

Purchased or Home-Grown

Reworking a Nursery Bonsai

You have the right to ask whether or not an expensive bonsai should be absolutely finished when it is sold. Every bonsai that is exported from Japan has been given a basic shape and is just as well formed as older, valuable plants. But you can do even more on your own using a series of artistic "tricks." These efforts will further improve both the details and the total appearance of your tree. Sometimes there are un-thought-of possibilities in the more modestly priced trees.

Foliage

Because the bonsai have been transported end to end in crates, carefully wired branches and twigs can be displaced—sometimes a lot, sometimes just a little. The sellers will generally do what they can to remedy the situation. But in a large group of trees, it is easy to overlook something. It is up to you to bring out the plant's designated shape, or to correct it until you are satisfied with its interest and har- mony. For example, you can easily achieve the stair-step effect in Japanese white pine branches, by bending the limbs down and allowing their branches to grow upward.

If wire is beginning to bind the bark in some places, or if it is rusted, you'll have to remove it quickly. Although the bonsai shouldn't be wired again immedi- ately, you can still train it a little using cord or even a little wire.

Because of their fast growth rate, deciduous trees can some- times look a little disheveled and neglected, especially if they haven't been regularly groomed by the dealers. Cut the long, spiky growths back far enough so that they will grow nicely into the shape of the foliage. Look at your tree critically and decide which branches might distort the overall appearance and have to be re- moved. Thin out places that have

Purchased or Home-Grown

Japanese maple *(Acer palmatum)*, approximately 50 years old. Oval, glazed dish,
22 × 16 inches (55 × 40 cm). Height,
42 inches (105 cm).

grown in too thickly, to achieve greater transparency.

Trunk
Take off the stumps of branches with a sharp knife—or turn them into artistic *jin.*

Roots
Sometimes during repotting, the all-important exposed roots are forgotten. A trunk should never be allowed to simply stick into the earth like a pole. It needs a harmonious transition. Use a wooden stick and the spray bottle of water to carefully uncover the roots. You may have to cut off a few little root hairs growing higher up on the trunk. Never dig too deeply into the root ball, however, even if there aren't any other roots to expose.

Pot
If your newly acquired bonsai is planted in one of the commonly used universal pots that doesn't suit its size or shape, don't hesitate to buy one that can considerably improve the tree's appearance. Move the tree from one pot into the other without allowing the root ball to fall apart. This falling apart can easily happen if the plant has been newly imported or potted.

A Guide to Cultivating

Needle Evergreens

Pinus parviflora pentaphylla
Japanese white pine

The Japanese white pine is without a doubt the best loved of all bonsai plants. There are a number of different varieties to choose from, including those with silver, gold, dark, or pale needles, which can be long, bending, short, thin, or straight. There is a whole range of bark types from fine to rough. The best kind for bonsai is one with a finely textured bark and thickly growing needles with a silvery white stripe. These trees are naturally inclined to dwarfed growth and often grow branches with short interspaces between the nodes. The Japanese white pine has an elegant, almost graceful habit, which the Japanese describe as a "feminine appearance."

Propagation and Training
Because of the Japanese white pine's very slow growth, grafting is used to speed up the process. Propogation by seed or cuttings take a lot of patience; collecting them in the wild outside of Japan is out of the question.

Determining a Style
Japanese white pines are excellent for any style. Wiring or training with cord should occur in winter.

Care and Pruning
The plant should be set in full sun, but given abundant water. Frequent spraying in summer is also especially important. Fertilizing should be done once in spring and again in fall, with the addition of one tablespoon of powdered horn or rapeseed. In spring, when the young candles appear, let them grow unhindered or shorten them in designated places by twisting or even cutting them off where branches should occur. In any case, don't allow several shoots from a single point to grow undisturbed. Instead, remove all the rest, leaving 1 or possibly 2. The first year after importing or after re-potting, the candles may grow a little long and the needles may not be as short as usual.

In the fall, without warning, portions of the needles will turn yellow and can be carefully removed. At the same time or the following spring, pruning of superfluous branches can be undertaken.

Repotting
Every 3 or 4 years. Older plants less often. The right time is in spring. A loamy ground with about 30 percent sand is optimum. Press it down firmly.

the Most Popular Bonsai Plants

Japanese white pine *(Pinus parviflora pent-phylla),* approximately 40 years old. Glazed ceramic pot, 14½×10 inches (36×25 cm). Total height, 25 inches (65 cm).

A Guide to Cultivating

Pinus thunbergii
Japanese black pine

Japanese black pines are almost as well loved in Japan as the white pines. Generally, their needles are a good bit longer and thicker. For many an advanced bonsai lover, their artistic habit is a quality that makes black pines especially valuable. Another aspect of the beauty of this plant lies in the distinctive texture of its trunk, especially the variety "contorta." The older this tree gets, the more fantastic and bizarre is the appearance of the thick, corky bark, a priceless attribute.

Propagation and Care
Digging plants out of the mountains seems ideal. Though we don't have the same varieties as those found in Japan, we have plants similar in appearance. Otherwise seeding or cutting is necessary.

Determining a Style
Formal upright or informal upright styles are best suited to Japanese black pine. When using wire or cord, exceptional caution is required that the bark doesn't break off. The best time to wire is right before the new buds break in early spring.

Care and Pruning
The Japanese black pine needs full sun and should be kept moist. Give the whole plant a good shower and additional spraying when it's very hot.

Fertilizing is similar to that of the Japanese white pine, but can be done 3 times per year because of its vigorous rate of growth. Prune buds in spring as soon as they develop. They should be completely removed; many new ones will appear at the same spot a few weeks later, which have smaller growth potential.

Limbs and branches should be shortened in March or September. In the fall pull off any unattractive growth.

Repotting
The same rules hold for the black pine as for the white: When it is young, root-prune every 3 years. Later on, intervals of five years are recommended so that the needles don't grow too big.

Pests
Young black pines are sometimes bothered by red spider mites, caterpillars, and aphids. Use insecticide in weak concentration.

the Most Popular Bonsai Plants

Japanese black pine *(Pinus thunbergii)*, approximately 25 years old. Glazed ceramic pot, 14½ × 11 inches (36 × 28 cm). Total height, 25 inches (65 cm).

A Guide to Cultivating

Picea glehnii
(P. jezoensis, P. sitchensis)
Spruces

Spruce trees are especially suited
for bonsai are recognizable by their
slow growth, unusually fine and
thick foliage, as well as rough or
interesting bark. Slow growth is a
result of the evolutionary process
in cold climates.

Propagation and Care
This is another case of where
good, stunted raw material may be
found in the hills. Air-layering
takes—compared to pines—only
about a half year. With good warm
temperatures and high humidity,
cuttings up to 6 inches (15 cm)
long can be taken.

Determining a Style
There are numerous possibilities.
Groups or forests work well. Wiring
can be undertaken in winter or
even earlier on younger branches.

Care and Pruning
Like the pines, the best situation is
full sun.
    When the buds swell in spring,
water a little less. In summer give
abundant water. Spray the entire
plant frequently.
    Fertilize just like pines.

Pruning the shoots should be
done weekly, so they don't get
long and spiky, but branch finely.
Prune wood in the winter.

Repotting
Young plants should be repotted
every 2 years; thereafter, not so often. The best time is April.

the Most Popular Bonsai Plants

Cryptomeria japonica
Cryptomeria

Somewhat rare outside of Japan, Cryptomeria is one of the most important bonsai plants. The tree makes a powerful impression, is resistant to disease, and distinguishes itself by small, thickly set needles, fine branching, and an attractive, rough bark. The color of the foliage changes with the seasons.

Propagation and Training
Normally, propagation is achieved by seeds or cuttings, with the cuttings requiring about 3 years.

You can, however, find your own substitute in a mountainous landscape. Look for one that has especially tiny needles that, although totally unrelated to Japanese cryptomeria, is just as promising.

Determining a Style
Because of its stately appearance and its thick trunk, the formal upright style is strongly recommended.

Care and Pruning
Protect the plant from full sun and hard frost, fertilizing it several times during the growing season. New shoots should be regularly trimmed with the fingertips when they are 1 inch (1 to 2 cm) long. Cut back limbs and branches in spring before they send out new shoots.

Repotting
Repot every 2 to 4 years in spring using a mixture of 50 percent loam, 30 percent sand, and 20 percent humus.

A special tip: You can either dig your fir tree out of the wild or buy it from a nursery. Find one that is too high for normal bonsai and simply cut away and the top to form a *jin*; another branch will then take over as leader.

A Guide to Cultivating

Juniperus chinensis
Chinese juniper

Juniperus rigida
Needle juniper

Chinese juniper has a long history of bonsai training. Its outstanding characteristics are little bushlike clusters of leaves and exfoliating bark. Among the numerous varieties of Chinese juniper, only the variety *J. chinensis sargentii* is really suitable for bonsai.

The needle juniper is only seldom used for bonsai, and gets its name from the short, thin needles with their light striping.

Propagation and Care
The best examples were dug out of the wild in Japan and then culti-

vated as bonsai when the plants were more than a hundred years old. For the most part, one has to use cuttings. Air-layering only works with the needle juniper.

Determining a Style
The Chinese juniper may be trained in any style imaginable: clasped-to-stone, informal upright, strongly

Chinese juniper *(Juniperus chinensis)*, approximately 20 years old, ceramic pot, 14½ × 11 inches (36 × 25 cm). Total height, 18 inches (45 cm).

curved trunk, and cascades are some favorites.

Needle junipers, because of their especially strong trunk, do well in the upright forms. Wire in February and March.

Care and Pruning

Both trees need a very bright and airy situation. The shortening of shoots should be done regularly throughout the year—especially with the Chinese juniper. Don't use scissors on the scaly leaves. Fingertips work much better.

Junipers sometimes suddenly send out new shoots on old wood. These shoots should be removed immediately, because doing it later will leave big scars.

the Most Popular Bonsai Plants

Once in a while Chinese junipers suddenly develop leaves that resemble those of the needle juniper. When this happens it is a sign that the plant is weakened and should be repotted or fertilized.

Repotting
Repot in March or April, shortly before the new shoots appear. The Chinese juniper grows well in a mixture of 30 percent sand and 70 percent loam, while the needle juniper should have the percentages reversed. Both types need frequent spraying after they have been repotted.

Warning
Fertilize only in very greatly diluted liquid forms. Otherwise growth will be uncontrollable. Feeding a few times in spring and in fall should suffice.

Chamaecyparis obtusa
Hinoki cypress

The Japanese dwarf false cypresses, often seen in our gardens, are very slow growing. They have a fine and dense foliage shading from green to a luminous gold (called sunny cypress).

Propagation and Training
Propagation is done by seeds or cuttings; nurseries also carry many interesting plants.

Determining a Style
Suitable styles include mainly clasped-to-stone plantings and the single tree trained in the broom style. Wire in spring.

Care and Pruning
Water abundantly, allowing no hot summer midday sun. Fertilizing, similar to that of junipers, should be in liquid form.

Prune shoots with fingernails several times in springs and fall. Thin out limbs and branches regularly every spring.

Repotting
Repot every 2 years in spring in a mixture of 50 percent loam, 30 percent sand, and 20 percent humus.

Needle juniper *(Juniperus rigida),* approximately 50 years old. Oval ceramic dish, 16×12 inches (40×30 cm). Total height, 29 inches (73 cm).

A Guide to Cultivating

Thuja orientalis
Oriental arborvitae

The oriental tree of life with its scaley leaves resembles the false cypress. It has the same capacity for dwarfing.

Propagation
Propagation is done by seed and cutting.

Determining a Style
The tree makes a majestic and thoroughly elegant impression planted singly in a formal upright style or lightly curved trunk. Like the Chinese juniper, with age parts of the bark exfoliate revealing the pale wood beneath. Train in early spring using wire.

Care and Pruning
The tree is quite drought-, cold-, and heat-resistant. However, its roots are sensitive to standing water. Water moderately and protect the plant from uninterrupted days of rain. Fertilize in spring and in fall. Shorten the shoots 3 times a year with the fingernails. Prune branches in fall.

Repotting
Repot every 2 to 4 years in spring using a mixture of 70 percent loam and 30 percent sand.

Deciduous Trees

Acer palmatum
Japanese maple

Acer buergerianum
Trident maple

In Japan, the Japanese maple is almost as well loved as the pines or the apricots for bonsai culture. The variety, *Atropurpureum,* is incredibly beautiful. Because of its fine texture and attractive color, the trunk of the plant is an attraction all by itself.

Buerger's maple is similar to the Japanese maple in many details, but has 3-lobed leaves. Both plants are robust and can endure great cold and drought.

Propagation and Training
The possibilities are many—ranging from cuttings and grafting to ground and air-layering. Interesting but expensive plants are found in nurseries.

Japanese maple, *(Acer palmatum)*, approximately 25 years old. The variety *Atropurpureum* has red leaves in February when they are new. Oval, glazed ceramic pot, 14×10 inches (35×25 cm). Total height, 29 inches (72 cm).

A Guide to Cultivating

Determining a Style

These trees are suitable for both
the formal upright and informal
upright styles. They are especially
beloved as clasped-to-stone
plantings.

Care and Pruning

A sunny and airy situation is ideal
for both trees, which benefit from
daily watering in summer. Water
the whole tree—even the leaves.

Fertilize in spring when the
leaves develop. Cut shoots back
regularly to the first or second pair
of leaves. Branch pruning should
be undertaken in spring. Use the
leaf-cutting method.

Repotting

The growth of shoots and roots is
rampant. Even so, you shouldn't
repot too often. With adequate root
pruning, every third year should
suffice.

Use a soil mix of 80 percent
loam and 20 percent sand.

Warning

The bark is quite sensitive. Wire
should be plastic-coated or wrapped in paper.

Japanese white pine *(Pinus pentaphylla),*
around 20 years old. Ceramic pot,
13×9 inches (32×23 cm). Total height,
29 inches (72 cm).

A Guide to Cultivating

Zelkova serrata
Japanese zelkova

Ulmus parviflora (Zelkova nire)
Japanese elm

Japanese zelkovas have an exceptionally fine-textured bark and the most densely developed scaffolding of all bonsai plants. They are therefore most attractive in winter. *Zelkova nire* has much smaller leaves than *Zelkova serrata,* which are lightly red when they appear. It also has a somewhat rougher bark and grows more slowly.

Propagation and Care
This is done by seed and cuttings.

Determining a Style
Every conceivable form is possible but the plant's natural habit lends itself wonderfully to the formal upright and broom styles. All wires should be wrapped in paper or plastic coated and removed early to avoid cutting into the bark.

Many Japanese bonsai books recommend not wiring any woody growth because this process seems to diminish the tree's energy.

Care and Pruning
Zelkovas should have a sunny situation with plenty of water and frequent showers. Never expose these plants to cold winds or frost. Because of their fast growth, they should be fertilized throughout the spring and summer.

A constant cutting back to the first or second leaf of each new shoot is important. The goal of your pruning should be a dense, evenly thick foliage. Branches and twigs can be trimmed or removed at any time. Leaf cutting is highly recommended.

Repotting
Repot in the same manner as maples. The soil should be predominantly loam with perhaps 10 percent sand and humus.

Japanese zelkova *(Zelkova serrata),* approximately 50 years old. Oval, glazed ceramic dish, 19×12 inches (43×29 cm). Total height, 22 inches (55 cm).

A Guide to Cultivating

Carpinus japonica
Japanese hornbeam

Fagus crenata
Beech

In Japan, beeches trained as bonsai are very special; in our native forests, great numbers of plants suitable for bonsai culture are waiting to be discovered. The beech's bark is bewitchingly beautiful. Another of this tree's excellent traits is its tendency to hang onto its red-brown leaves all winter long until the emergence of the new buds in spring.

Propagation and Training
Seeding or air-layering are the traditional methods. Nurseries carry many interesting varieties.

Determining a Style
The best styles for the beeches are forests, clasped-to-stone, or formal upright single-tree styles.

Wire used for training should be wrapped in paper and may be left in place no longer than half a year because of the quick rate of branch growth. Wiring should be undertaken in March.

Care and Pruning
Give abundant water; don't allow the plant to sit too long in the hot sun. Protect the smallest branches from frost.

Fertilize between May and September when the tree is actively growing. Prune shoots no more than 2 or 3 times annually. Leaf-cutting techniques can be used in alternate years; shorten branches and twigs when you repot.

Repotting
Because these trees are such strong growers, repotting should be done every spring. Make a clean, diagonal cut through the thick taproot underneath the tree. Use a mix of about 50 percent loam and sand.

Notice
The instructions for care listed above may be used on oaks.

Hornbeam *(Carpinus laxiflora)*, approximately 35 years old. Oval, glazed dish, 26×16 inches (65×40 cm). Total height, 40 inches (100 cm).

A Guide to Cultivating

Betula tauschii
Birch

The birch is a tree whose familiar small leaves, attractive catkins, and last but not least, outstanding bark, are well loved. It makes a very interesting bonsai plant.

Propagation and Care
Birches are grown from seed.

Determining a Style
Leaning styles, informal upright, or the broom style suit the birch. They also do well in groups, in which very young plants can play an important role.

Care and Pruning
Always take great care to supply adequate water; in addition, on hot days the leaves should be sprayed and the entire plant should be protected from the hot midday sun. From May throughout the summer, use a fertilizer—preferably liquid. Prune back to the first or second leaf regularly. After late summer, prune less and less often until winter, when a single final pruning will suffice.

Repotting
Repot every 1 to 2 years in April using a mixture of 80 percent loam and 20 percent sand.

Salix babylonica
Weeping willow

Willows are used as bonsai only infrequently—yet their unusual habit and catkins are quite attractive.

Propagation and Training
Willows are usually grown from cuttings.

Determining a Style
Informal upright, leaning, or cascade styles are suitable.

Care and Pruning
The willow grows faster than any other woody plant and requires enormous water supplies to support its growth. It should, therefore, not have too much sun and be thoroughly and abundantly watered. Fertilize throughout the summer into September using nutrient-rich fertilizer cubes or a very rich liquid fertilizer administered monthly.

Cut back radically when repotting.

Repotting
The root growth in willows is so rampant that they may eventually require 2 prunings per year—in spring and again in midsummer. Use a soil mix of 80 percent loam and 20 percent sand.

the Most Popular Bonsai Plants

Morus alba
Mulberry

In the Far East, the mulberry is well known as a source of food for silkworms. Frequently seen in southern Europe, the mulberry is hardy to zone 4 in the United States.

Propagation and Training
Mulberries are grown from seed.

Determining a Style
Styles usually used are the formal upright, the leaning, and the half-cascade. Wire when transplanting, Use either paper-wrapped or plastic-coated wire for the mulberry's sensitive bark.

Care and Pruning
Always water copiously and never allow the tree to dry out. Protect it from strong direct sunlight when the root ball is dry.

Fertilize from spring until summer. Cut back branches in March or April, shortening new shoots regularly before they reach an inch (1 cm) in length.

Repotting
Repot every 1 to 2 years in spring. The soil mixture should be 70 percent loam and 30 percent sand/humus.

Rhus succedanae
Sumac

Sumacs are used infrequently in this country for two reasons. Some are not winter-hardy, and others may cause an allergic reaction in some people. In the Orient they have been used for centuries as a source of lacquer, made from their milky sap.

Determining a Style
Formal or informal upright styles, and half-cascades suit the sumac. Wrap the wire with paper and wire in March. New branches may be wired in summer.

Care and Pruning
Keep well watered in summer to avoid drying out the root ball. Cut back regularly to the second or third leaf, as soon as the shoots are about an inch long. In spring fertilize with a liquid several times or use fertilizer cubes. Remove the fertilizer cube in the fall.

Repotting
Depending upon the age of the plant, repot every 1 to 2 years in spring. The soil mix should be 70 percent loam and 30 percent sand/humus.

A Guide to Cultivating

Ginkgo biloba
Ginkgo

Ginkgo is a legendary tree—one of the most unusual on earth. Botanists aren't really sure whether to place it with the deciduous trees or the conifers. Its leaves, fan shaped with numerous veins, turn shining gold in the winter.

Firethorn *(Pyracantha angustifolia),* approximately 10 years old. Ceramic pot, 13×10 inches (32×27 cm). Total height, 16 inches (40 cm).

Propagation and Care
Ginkgos are propagated by seed, cuttings, and air-layering. You can also find them in one of the larger nurseries. Simply cut back and let it send out new shoots.

Determining a Style
The formal upright style is best.

Care and Pruning
Protect against hot sun. Water and fertilize abundantly. From spring into summer, surplus shoots should be removed and other ones shortened. Regularly thin out branches each spring for appearance's sake, but make sure the tree isn't stunted by too much cutting back.

Repotting
Repot once a year in spring when the new shoots appear. Use a mixture of 80 percent loam and 20 percent sand.

the Most Popular Bonsai Plants

Blooming and Fruit-Bearing Plants

The following plants included here are cherished because of their blooms and/or fruits, and are suitable for bonsai cultivation. Many fruit-bearing bonsai have to have their fruits thinned. An overabundant harvest would seriously weaken the tree. Other types bear such enormous fruits that they ruin the bonsai's miniature picture.

A Guide to Cultivating

Cotoneaster horizontalis
Rockspray

Cotoneaster is a broadleaf ever-green, frequently planted as an ornamental.

Propagation and Training
Normally, propagation is done by seed or cuttings. Air-layering or heading will provide faster results.

Determining a Style
Rockspray is suited to an informal upright or clasped-to-stone style.

Care and Pruning
In order to have fruit, the plant needs regular fertilizing from spring into the fall. Good air circulation and abundant water and an un-glazed pot to prevent the growth fungi are also necessary.

Repotting
Repot once each year in early spring because of the fast root growth. Use a mixture of 70 per-cent loam and 30 percent sand.

Ilex serrata
Finetooth holly

Ilex as a bonsai is a great favorite because of the crop of coral red berries and the beauty of its finely textured trunk. In winter as well this bonsai hangs onto its berries and is enormously attractive.

Propagation and Training
Ilex is usually propagated by seed. You can also try cultivating a nursery plant.

Determining a Style
The informal upright, the wind-blown, or the cascading forms are suitable.

Care and Pruning
Never, never neglect watering or your tree may not produce its at-tractive berry crop. A number of kinds of hollies are not winter-har-dy and have to be brought into an unheated, frost-free room in Oc-tober.
Fertilize from spring into the sum-mer. All shoots should be immedi-ately removed to provide a dense, compact shape. Unnecessary branches can be removed when the holly is repotted. Wire new shoots the summer after they appear. Special care should be taken when wiring due to the brittleness of the branches.

the Most Popular Bonsai Plants

Repotting
Repot in spring before the shoots appear. The soil should be almost entirely loam.

Warning
Bearing fruit uses a lot of the tree's energy. It is possible that a tree weakened by bearing a large crop of berries may have scarcely any the following year. In order to avoid this situation, you can remove the berries after they have adorned the plant for a month.

Wisteria floribunda
Wisteria

Wisterias are basically vining, climbing plants that are suitable for bonsai if the vines can be kept short. The plant's special appeal is the appearance of long, drooping flower clusters in white, pink, or violet.

Propagation
Wisterias are grafted.

Determining a Style
The informal upright and especially the cascade forms are perfect for this vining plant. Wiring should be undertaken in spring when the buds appear.

Care and Pruning
After the plant has bloomed in the spring, fertilize heavily until July. Then let the plant dry out until the tips of leaves droop a few times—then water well again. This method should hinder the plant's production of foliage, and potential leaf buds will produce flowers instead. Keep the plant evenly moist. Cut leaf stems only after they have hardened. Branches may be cut back or removed entirely right after the flowers fade.

After blooming, a great number of fruits develop. Remove a good portion of these promptly so that they do not weaken the bonsai.

Repotting
Repot each year right after blooming. The composition of the soil should be 80 percent loam and 20 percent humus.

A Guide to Cultivating

Prunus mume
Japanese flowering apricot

In the United States, apricot bonsai are somewhat rare, but in Japan they are among the most popular.

Propagation and Training
Apricots are propagated by cuttings and grafts.

Determining a Style
The best styles are more or less curving, informal upright styles. Wiring—if it's necessary at all—should be done in summer. Use nothing but plastic-coated or paper-wrapped wire for the apricot's extremely sensitive bark.

Care and Pruning
These plants need abundant water and fertilizer during their growth period.

Unnecessary new shoots should be removed immediately and others should have—at the very least—their tips removed in order not to grow too long. Pruning may not be too heavy or the tree won't bloom at all. After the flowers fade, take off the wilted buds in order to nip fruit production in the bud.

Repotting
Repot after the flowers fade once each year in a mixture of 60 percent loam, 20 percent sand, 20 percent humus.

Red, blooming peach, about 5 to 7 years old. Glazed, ceramic pot, 5½ inches (14 cm). Total height, 16 inches (40 cm).

A Guide to Cultivating

Chaenomeles lagenaria
Quince

This naturally shrubby tree makes a superb bonsai with its beautiful spring blossoms. A few types also develop interesting fruit.

Propagation and Training
Quince is propagated by cuttings and grafting and may—with a bit of skill—be grown by division.

Determining a Style
The style should suit the nature of the quince, a low plant with a curving, knotty trunk. Because of the vigorous shoot growth, many types of quinces may be trained by a single rigorous pruning, without any need for wire.

Care and Pruning
Water abundantly and spray frequently, especially before the flower buds open. Shield from the afternoon summer sun. Fertilize from spring until fall while the tree is actively growing.

Shorten or completely remove young shoots as soon as they appear. These will be followed by new shoots. Leave the new ones alone until fall and then prune again.

Repotting
Repot in spring or fall in a mixture of 75 percent loam and 25 percent sand. Handle the Chinese quince *(Chaenomeles sinensis)* the same way, with one exception: It can be cut back several times and the fruits may be left on the tree until they are completely ripe.

the Most Popular Bonsai Plants

Jasminum nudiflorum
Winter jasmine

One of the best-loved flowering bonsai in Japan, this jasmine blooms in winter with wondrously fragrant yellow blossoms. It becomes more precious as it ages, with its bark turning marvelously gnarled. Unfortunately, winter jasmine is difficult to find in nurseries.

Determining a Style
Grow winter jasmine alone, in an informal or formal upright style; wire after pruning and do not fail to wrap the wire with paper. All branches are particularly brittle.

Care and Cutting
See quince.

Repotting
Repot either before bloom in early spring or in fall after the leaves drop. Use 2 parts loam and 1 part coarse sand for a mix. Handle the following in the same way:

- *Prunus donarium*
  Japanese wild cherry
- *Malus spontanea*
  Wild apple
- *Punica granatum*
  Pomegranate
- *Pyrus serotina*
  Japanese pear
- *Pyracantha angustifolia*
  Firethorn

All of the above listed require some winter protection. Depending upon conditions, frost could damage anything from the smallest twigs to the entire plant.

Unusual Forms

Miniatures

Miniature (*mame*) bonsai occupy their own special niche in Japan. While a normal bonsai might reach a height of anywhere from 8 to 32 inches (20 to 80 cm), miniatures range from around 2 to 6 inches (5 to 15 cm) high. These dwarfs among the bonsai are very seldom found in collections. The reason is that after only a few years, with the development of a thick trunk and branches, there isn't any room for even radical measures to be taken to maintain the minuscule form. The pots used are between 1 inch (2 cm) and—at most—4 inches (10 cm) large. Because of the limitations imposed by leaf size, the number of suitable plants is understandably minimal.

Not only keeping a plant alive, but trying to train it in a *mame* style requires enormous skill—especially when dealing with the smallest of the small. After a very short time, the tiny pot is choked with roots. The soil quickly loses its ability to provide water because the roots soak it up as quickly as it is given. On warm days, miniatures may never be set in the sun, because the danger of drying out and wilting is so great. Frequent spraying and a loamy soil help the water situation.

In order to achieve relatively natural proportions, the leaf-cutting method is absolutely necessary.

Repotting, along with a cautious root pruning, can and must occur each year.

A shelf of miniatures. Clockwise from top right: apricot, 8½ inches (21 cm), Japanese maple, 7½ inches (19 cm), Trident maple clasped-to-stone, 7½ inches (19 cm), cryptomeria, 8 inches (20 cm), Chinese juniper, 5½ inches (14 cm).

Unusual Forms

Giant Bonsai

In addition to the dwarfs among the bonsai, there are also giants. These are plants which are grown in pots and reach a height of between 3 and 6 feet. In ancient China interesting trees were dug out of the ground in the mountains in this way. Similarly, today relatively large trees in containers are cultivated in the same way as bonsai. They make superb specimen plants when used in a little courtyard or against a plain house wall. Don't hesitate to continue on with a bonsai that has grown too large, repotting it in gradually larger and larger pots. Plants from the wild can be ideal for this purpose, just as extremely small ones are for "normal" bonsai sizes.

A Bonsai Garden

Whoever thinks that all there is to bonsai is the cultivation of little trees has another thing to learn.

In little entrance gardens—as in the Japanese gardens traditionally laid out in large parks—fairy landscapes with their own different geographical areas and typical vegetation can be simulated. Larger shrubs and trees are trained in idealized forms using pruning and wiring, as well as stakes and poles.

For many this kind of cultivation may appear a little overdone or even kitschy, but such a garden can enchant even the most skeptical visitor. Artful lakes and hills are surrounded by flora: blooming azaleas and gnarled old giants of trees; mountainous landscapes give way to swampland. The secret of all this, a fundamental rule of bonsai, lies in a simple and unadorned elegance, in a perfection of form, illustrating the apparently random imperfection of "nature." Why shouldn't we, as we begin to understand bonsai, give in to the urge to try a totally different kind of garden design? The use of stones in different sizes and colors, the artful placing of beautiful and unusual nursery plants, and, finally, the year-round management and pruning isn't nearly so foreign seeming when you think that in the castle gardens of Europe many similar practices were carried out. In a tiny big-city garden, a few square yards of a Japanese-inspired garden might create on oasis of peace. An ocean of round pebbles surrounding a single boulder island makes a peaceful subject for meditation.

For a bonsai garden, you can use any existing plants that seem appropriate in form and size, or restyle the existing plants and add new ones. Don't begin with either too small or too fully grown trees. Instead try to slow down their rate of growth and make a goal, to achieve their basic form in two to three years through pruning. On the whole, training is the same as it is with the little bonsai—except, of course, for transplanting and potting. Train the lower branches of conifers to grow upward and thin them with the aid of a saw to give the impression of very much older, taller trees.

Unusual Forms

Bamboo and Herbaceous Bonsai

This section briefly describes another practice very similar to bonsai. It is used on plants not suitable for traditional bonsai. Bamboo is a common ornamental in Japanese gardens, and sooner or later it was bound to be "bonsaied." Of course, very different methods have to be employed for a very different kind of woody growth. Small groups or forests of dwarf bamboo give the illusion of a seaside grove when arranged with stone in a flat, wide dish with a little pond. Indeed, bamboo is carefree. It needs abundant water and fertilizer throughout the year and can be cut back to the ground in spring if it has grown too tall the previous year. Otherwise, pluck out the tallest central shoots to control growth. Occasional dried reeds and leaves enhance and enrich the overall appearance and should be left alone for a while. You can find varieties of dwarf bamboo in good nurseries. To propagate, simply divide.

Herbaceous bonsai are another manifestation of the Japanese genius for arranging plants. In place of trees and shrubs, herbaceous plants, grasses, ferns, and moss are used. These plants are grown in arrangements of either the characteristic form of a single type—or in combinations. Augmented by an interesting stone or a piece of dried wood, these arrangements express simply and impressively the beauty and quality of the plant in different seasons against a natural backdrop. A suitable size and habit is required to complement the pot for a harmonious overall appearance. No list of suitable plants will be given here, so that your own imagination will not be limited by suggestion.

Sooner or later anyone who gets involved with traditional bonsai styles will gravitate toward the occasional special arrangement of herbaceous bonsai. From there it's just a short step to another Japanese specialty, ikebana.

Unusual Forms

Bamboo bonsai.

Unusual Forms

Saikei

This is the place to say something about another relatively young branch of Japanese garden art. Saikei means something like "living landscape." Using bonsai methods, segments of landscapes are reproduced with little trees, grasses, mosses, stones, and sand. These are arranged on wide, flat dishes. Saikei came about after World War II in the wake of the general popularizing of bonsai.

Clasped-to-stone plantings and forests had become more and more admired and coveted. Incorporating these two styles, the saikei form emerged. At the same time, saikei adopted a number of traditional bonsai rules while discarding others. Yet, there are concrete differences between bonsai and saikei clasped-to-stone and group plantings. Whereas a bonsai forest is always composed of many trees of the same type of nearly the same age and relatively unified in type, saikei includes very young plants of different kinds. With clasped-to-stone, a good bonsai stone is hard to find, because it has to complement the plant in shape, size, color, and texture. (Lately specialty stores carry bonsai rocks, ideally suited to the purpose, but often nearly as costly as the bonsai itself.) Saikei uses every possible stone type. Any unattractive parts are simply hidden by covering with earth. Saikei embraces several other refreshing notions.

- Because bonsai's strict rules have been reinterpreted, there is room for experimentation. The freedom of movement allows for more creativity.
- Saikei raw material can be found anywhere and bought cheaply. Dishes are generally plain and simple; indeed, anyone who wanted to could make his own. Besides clay, wood is an appropriate material, if it is treated with preservative. Stones to plant or decorate the landscape can be found in any field. Plants can be quite young; if, after a few years, they grow out of proportion to the landscape, simply replace them with others and cultivate them as bonsai.
- Saikei enriches the bonsai hobby. If young plants have spent a few years in saikei arrangements before becoming bonsai, they are doubly esteemed.
- Success comes quicker when constructing a saikei landscape than it will with growing a bonsai. Saikei also allows for rearranging plants, replacing some, taking out a hill here, building another hill there, and so on.

Unusual Forms

- In addition to all of the other attributes that make saikei freer and more spontaneously creative, there is also the potent argument that the layman needn't have the fear of damaging a valuable tree through ignorance of its proper maintenance. If you start with economical young plants, you will learn how to handle them over time. Basically the techniques of saikei and bonsai care only differ superficially.

Perhaps the most negative aspect of saikei lies in its potential for kitsch. After an elite, centuries-old bonsai culture that used a rigidly traditional system of rules, the saikei idea thumbs its nose at tradition in allowing the greatest possible freedom. This is fine. But there is a certain danger in twisting the original idea of bonsai. All manner of unnecessary products are available for saikei arrangements: little statues of working peasants, little dogs and birds, houses, bridges, and stone lanterns—all scaled to miniature landscapes. There are even complete imitations—not for clarifying bonsai principles—but for use as kitschy fairy landscapes.

Bonsai Terms

For those readers who will eventually venture further into the art of bonsai, the following list of terms may prove helpful. It includes plant names, style names, and other related terms. It would not only be confusing, but be ridiculous, to include words whose very pronunciation was beyond our grasp.

Plants

goyo matsu	Japanese white pine, *Pinus parviflora pentaphylla*
hinoki	False cypress, *Chamaecyparis obtusa*
kaedi	Trident maple, *Acer buergerianum*
keyake	Zelkova, *Zelkova serrata*
konote kashiwa	Arborvitae, *Thuja orientalis*
kuro matsu	Japanese black pine, *Pinus thunbergii*
momiji	Japanese maple, *Acer palmatum*
shimpaku	Chinese juniper, *Juniperus chinensis*
sugi	Cryptomeria, *Cryptomeria japonica*
tosho	Juniper, *Juniperus rigida*
beni shitan	Rockspray, *Cotoneaster horizontalis*
boke	Quince, *Chaenomeles lagenaria*
buna	Beech, *Fagus crenata*
fuji	Wisteria, *Wisteria floribunda*
icho	Ginkgo, *Ginkgo biloba*
kumashide	Japanese hornbeam, *Carpinus japonica*
nire	Little leaf zelkova, *Zelkova nire*
obai	Winter jasmine, *Jasminum nudiflorum*
ume	Japanese apricot, *Prunus mume*
umemodoki	Finetooth holly, *Ilex serrata*

Bonsai Terms

Styles

bunjingi	literary style, very high branches
chokkan	formal upright tree
fukinagashi	windblown style
hokidachi	broom style
han kengai	half-cascade style
ikadabuki	a group of one kind of trees
ishitsuki	clasped-to-stone style
kabudachi	several trees growing from one root
kengai	cascade style
moyogi or *bankan*	informal upright, curving trunk
negari	root trunk form, the tree grows on high surface roots
netsuranari	the raft style
shakan	bending trunk
sokan	double-trunk style
yose ue	forest style

Types of Soil

akatsuchi	red loam
arakida tsuchi	earth from under rice fields
fuyodo	humus and woodland soil
goro tsuchi	coarsely grained earth
kanuma tsuchi	light clay with sand
keto tsuchi	turf
kuropoka	loose, dark loamy soil
kuro tsuchi	black loam
tenjingawa suna	a type of river sand

Bonsai Terms

General Terms

daiki	root stock
eda zashi	branch pruning
gobo ne	taproot
hamizu	spraying leaves with water, misting
hariganikate	wiring the branches
ha zashi	leaf cutting
hige ne	root hairs
honbachi	genuine bonsai dish
kabuwake	propagation by division
misho	propagation by seed
moto tsugi	grafting stock
ne zashi	root pruning
sashi ho	cutting
sashiki	planting a cutting
seishi	styling
sentei	cutting back
shinme zashi	shoot pruning
suiban	flat tablet without drainage holes
tekishin	shoot cutting
ten tsugi	scion
toriki	air-layering
tsugiki	grafting
yamadori	collecting plants in the wild

Bonsai Societies

American Bonsai Society
Box 358
Keene, New Hampshire 03431

Bonsai Clubs International
800 West Virginia Street #501
Tallahassee, Florida 32304

Index

Air-layering, 30–31
Age, 15
Aphids, 44
Apricot, 105
Arborvitae, 90

Back side of bonsai, 60
Bamboo, 112
Bark, 14
Basic shape, 60
Beech, 96
Broom style, 50
Birch, 98
Blooming bonsai, 101–107
Bonsai gardens, 110–11
Branch, 14
Broom style, 50
Buerger's maple, 90

Cascade style, 58
Care, 15
China, 10
Chinese juniper, 86
Clasped-to-stone style, 52
Clump style, 54
Collecting, 19
Cold treatment, 23
Cord, 66
Correcting shape, form, 61
Cotoneaster, 102
Containers, 9, 31–32
Cuttings, 25–26

Diary, 16
Dishes, 31–32
Double-trunk style, 54
Dormant period, 41
Dwarf, 16–18

Elm, 94
Examples, natural, 10, 14

False cypress, 89
Fertilizers, 40
Finetooth holly, 102–103
Fir, 85

Flowering quince, 106
Foliage, 14
Forest style, 56
Front, 60

Germination period, 23
Giant bonsai, 110
Ginkgo, 100
Grafting, 28
Grafting scar, 28

Half-cascade style, 58
Herbaceous bonsai, 112
Hinoki cypress, 89
History, 10

Ilex, 102
Illness, 43
Informal upright style, 48
Investment, 74–75

Japan, 11
Japanese black pine, 82
Japanese elm, 94
Japanese hornbeam, 96
Japanese maple, 90
Japanese white pine, 80
Jasmine, 107
Juniper, 86

Leaf-cutting method, 69

Maples, 90–93
Minerals, 40
Miniatures, 109
Moss, 14, 38
Mulberry, 99
Multiple trunks, 54

Needle juniper, 86
Nursery plants, 21

Pests, 44
Philosophy, 11
Placing, 41–43
Pots, 14, 31–32

Index

Potting, 20, 34–38
Pruning, 9, 66–68

Quince, 106

Raft style, 56
Rare forms, 109
Religion, 11
Repotting, 34–38
Renovation, 77–79
Rock planting, 52
Rockspray, 102
Root rot, 43
Roots, 13
Rules, 13–14

Saikei, 114–15
Seed, propagation from, 23
Slanting style, 50
Soil, 9, 32, 33
Spruce, 84
Stratification, 23
Stunting, 10
Sumac, 99

Taproot, 35
Thinning, 60–61
Tools, 44–45
Training, 46
Training, duration of, 15
Trace elements, 40
Transplanting, 34–38
Trunk, 14

Upright style (formal), 48
Upright style (informal), 48

Value, 13–14

Watering, 38–40
Water supply, 10
Weakened condition, 43–44
Weeping willow, 98
Wind, 10
Windblown style, 51
Winter protection, 41
Wiring, 61–66
Wiring, unwinding, 65–66
Wisteria, 103

Zelkova, 94

Other Macmillan Gardening Guides are available
at your local bookstore or from
Macmillan Publishing Company

To order directly, mail the form below to:
MACMILLAN PUBLISHING COMPANY
Special Sales Department
866 Third Avenue
New York, NY 10022

	Quantity	ISBN	Title	Price	Total
1	_____	0020626606	**Bonsai**	$6.95	_____
2	_____	0020635206	**Orchids**	$6.95	_____
3	_____	0020633602	**Berry Gardening**	$6.95	_____
4	_____	0020631308	**Ornamental Gardening**	$6.95	_____
5	_____	0020631502	**Organic Gardening**	$6.95	_____
6	_____	0020631405	**Natural Herb Gardening**	$6.95	_____

Please add postage and handling costs—$1.00 for the first book and
50¢ for each additional book—and applicable state sales tax.

TOTAL $ _____

_____ Enclosed is my check/money order payable to Macmillan Publishing Co.

_____ Bill my _____ MasterCard _____ Visa Card #_____

Expiration date _____ Signature _____
—Charge orders valid only with signature—

                                                           Lines   Units

Control No. _____ T–Code _____ _____

Account Number/San _____ For charge orders only:

Ship to: _____ Bill To: _____

_____ _____

_____ _____

_____ Zip Code _____ ZipCode

For information regarding bulk purchases please write to Special Sales Director at the above
address. Publisher's prices are subject to change without notice. Offer good January 1,
1986 through December 31, 1986. Allow 3 weeks for delivery.

FC#274